Thomas Alfred Spalding

Federation and Empire

a Study in Politics

Thomas Alfred Spalding

Federation and Empire
a Study in Politics

ISBN/EAN: 9783743306493

Manufactured in Europe, USA, Canada, Australia, Japa

Cover: Foto ©ninafisch / pixelio.de

Manufactured and distributed by brebook publishing software (www.brebook.com)

Thomas Alfred Spalding

Federation and Empire

CONTENTS

INTRODUCTION:
    PAGE
  CHAPTER I.—The Constitutional Problem - - - 1
  CHAPTER II.—The Functions of Parliament - - - 10

THE FOUNDATIONS:

  CHAPTER III.—The Methods of Investigation - - 25
  CHAPTER IV.—The Limit of Legislative Capacity - 45
  CHAPTER V.—The Debating Function - - - - 64
  CHAPTER VI.—The Danger to the Constitution - - 83

THE BURDENS OF THE STATES:

  CHAPTER VII.—The Burden of England - - - 115
  CHAPTER VIII.—The Burden of Scotland - - - 126
  CHAPTER IX.—The Burden of Scotland *(continued)* - 144
  CHAPTER X.—The Burden of Scotland *(continued)* - 159
  CHAPTER XI.—The Burden of Ireland - - - 174
  CHAPTER XII.—The Burden of Ireland *(continued)* - 192
  CHAPTER XIII.—The Burden of Ireland *(continued)* - 207
  CHAPTER XIV.—The Lifting of the Burdens - - 224

THE NATURE OF FEDERATION:

  CHAPTER XV.—The Objections to Federation - - 241
  CHAPTER XVI.—The Balance of Gain and Loss - - 260
  CHAPTER XVII.—Federation *versus* Home Rule - - 291
  CHAPTER XVIII.—Conclusion - - - - - 303

I
INTRODUCTION

FEDERATION AND EMPIRE

CHAPTER I

THE CONSTITUTIONAL PROBLEM

The political problem which will be discussed in the following pages is one which affects the well-being of every inhabitant of the United Kingdom. It is, I believe, the supreme problem of the day: one which must perforce be solved ere long, and be solved by the nation. But it is difficult to induce people to consider this problem carefully, because it entails the examination of a number of questions which cannot be presented to them in an attractive form, and it is therefore difficult to persuade them that the national well-being is really involved in it. The mere mention of a "constitutional" question is apt to strike terror into the hearts of most men. They incline to the opinion that such matters are fit subjects for learned discussion amongst lawyers, but that the average elector should be content to vote blue or buff without wearying himself with theories which are, in all probability, the product of the bookworm or the pedant.

But our constitution is not the creation of lawyers, bookworms, or pedants. It has been built up, during the course of centuries, by the people. Slowly and silently, on the whole, it has been constructed, although its progress has been marked at intervals by conflict whenever privilege has found an interest in opposing its normal development. It is the embodiment of the national idea of the nation's political needs. It is growing still. Its great virtue is that it is capable of constant readaptation to the changing requirements of a progressive people.

Let us take an illustration of the way in which our constitution is growing. Suppose that, on opening our newspapers to-morrow morning, we should read an announcement that the Queen had intimated to the Premier that she had no longer any need for his services, and that she had entrusted some other statesman with the formation of a cabinet. We should say at once, "What nonsense! The ministry has not been defeated in the House of Commons. The thing can't be done." By that exclamation we should mean that the alleged action of the Crown was so palpably "unconstitutional" that we were convinced that the newspapers had been misinformed. But according to the "theory"—that is, the earlier practice—of the constitution, all ministers are "Servants of the Crown," and the Crown is entitled to dismiss them without giving them even a month's notice. At the end of the last century George III. told Pitt that if he were deprived of this prerogative, he should not deem the throne of Great Britain to be worth occupying.[1] William IV. actually exercised the prerogative in 1834, but the experiment did not prove a success.

How is it, then, that the action which was not only constitutional, but possible in 1834, has become both unconstitutional and impossible at the present day? It is because the electors, at the very first opportunity, sent the ministry which William IV. had constituted to the right-about; and since that time popular opinion has been so strongly opposed to the exercise of this particular prerogative that it has remained in abeyance. The modern doctrine that the existence of the Government depends solely upon the confidence of the House of Commons has taken its place. But that doctrine is not a written law. It is the outcome of practice and custom, which are followed because they are consonant with the wish of the nation.

This illustration will be enough to prove,

[1] "If the two only remaining privileges of the Crown are infringed—that of negativing bills which have been passed by both Houses of Parliament, and that of naming the ministers to be employed—I cannot but feel, as far as regards my person, that I can be no longer of any utility to this country, nor can with honour continue in this island."—Stanhope's "Life of Pitt," vol. 1, app., p. vi.

not only that our constitution is being constantly built up and remodelled, but also that those constitutional maxims which are not to be found in any authoritative document are, in absolute fact, created by the will of those whom the constitution controls. How much more is this true of those portions of the constitution which are to be found in statutes enacted by Parliament. The doctrine that no ordinance shall be legally binding which has not received the assent of the Commons through their representatives in Parliament is far more ancient than that to which reference has just been made. No change can be effected in this written law without such assent. If the machinery of government works badly because readaptation is necessary, the responsibility for the consequent evil rests upon the shoulders of every individual who, by his vote, is capable of aiding to bring about the needful change.

If, therefore, we, the citizens of the United Kingdom, are the sole makers of the constitution under which we live, it certainly behoves us to watch with constant and wary eyes the instrument through which our wishes find expression. If the functions of Parliament are not working smoothly, we may be sure that some evil will result to the body politic, for Parliament is the brain of the nation.

It is true that it has lately become the fashion

among certain unthoughtful persons to deny this. The denial sometimes takes exaggerated form in the assertion that, if Parliament were not to meet for a year, the nation would not be a penny the worse, perhaps would be many pence the better. Let us consider for a moment what such a proposal really means. If Parliament were not to meet this year, before the year was out we should have no army and no navy, because the special Act which controls the services would have lapsed, and because, even if there were enough money in the Government coffers to pay the cost of those services, such payment could not legally be made without an Appropriation Act. Our army would be disbanded, and our war-ships would lie, useless hulks, in the docks. Payment of the interest on the national debt could be made out of the income which does not depend upon annual Acts of Parliament,[1] but credit would nevertheless be shaken, commerce would be dislocated, and we should be on the eve of universal bankruptcy. Every man, woman and child would suffer, simply because Parliament had not met for a few months. The suspension, even for a short time, of the functions of Parliament would produce this paralysis. Is it not true, then, that Parliament is the brain of the nation?

[1] Under the National Debt and Local Loans Act, 1887, 50 Vict., c. 16.

Such a total paralysis is inconceivable. But even a partial paralysis, which prevented Parliament from fulfilling efficiently the legislative and administrative work of the nation, would be fraught with great danger. The immense social and material progress which the nation has made during the present century has created a continuing need for fresh legislation. Consider for a moment the new subjects with which Parliament has been busied during that period: education, police, the regulation of factories, questions of hygiene and urban and rural improvements, the complicated laws relating to railways, gas, water, and electric lighting, not to mention the grant of constitutions creating local autonomy in our larger colonies. These are only samples of the new subjects for legislation which have been opened up by our national progress.

And surely no one will contend that we have reached the end of this development; that the need for fresh legislation on new subjects, or for revising legislation on old ones, has now ceased. The contradiction of that contention is to be found in every newspaper that we read, in every political speech to which we listen. No statesman nowadays adjures us to rest and be thankful. Each has his panacea to recommend. The contention of political rivals invariably is, either that their opponents are legislating upon the wrong subject, or upon the right subject in the wrong fashion.

In fact, if we study the political world at all carefully, we are astonished at the multitude of questions which people are endeavouring to force upon the attention of Parliament. There never was a time in the whole of our history when men were so eager to open up new questions and to reconsider others which have long been deemed settled. It is a condition inseparable from national progress; perhaps it may even be found to be a cause of it.

But if we turn to Parliament itself, we find that for some years there has existed a discernible inability to deal effectually with the whole of the problems which one section or another desires to bring under its consideration. Ministers responsible for the national welfare bring forward, year after year, measures which they declare to be for the national benefit, and, year after year, withdraw a large number of those measures, solely on the ground that the House of Commons has no time to consider them. Groups of members who are eager to promote bills which they believe to be desirable are unable to obtain even an hour or two for the discussion of their proposals.

Now this is surely a great evil. It is not contended that all these bills should be passed, but that it is a misfortune that they cannot be considered. Much proposed legislation would, after undergoing the ordeal of discussion, disappear into the region of exposed absurdity; but the man with a grievance which he cannot ventilate is a man with a double grievance. The safety-valve for grievances is full and speedy discussion.

This inability to deal effectually with all, or even a reasonable proportion of the measures which are brought forward, is what I have ventured to term the partial paralysis of Parliament. It is to be feared that this paralysis is increasing: that Parliament is year by year accumulating arrears of work which it cannot overtake. We are face to face with an evil which will grow worse the longer it is neglected. If Parliament lags behind the needs of the nation, the time will come when it will fall into disrepute and contempt, and men will ask one another why they suffer it.

The glib answer usually given to any inquiry as to the cause of this paralysis is that it is due to the increasing loquacity of members of the House of Commons, and to the invention of the art of obstruction. The two answers are practically one, because loquacity is the chief instrument of obstruction. But we must be careful lest we confound effect with cause. It is remarkable that the paralysis of Parliament should be occasioned by the increase of loquacity precisely during the period in which the House of Commons was placing the most stringent limits upon superfluous talk. May it not rather be that the over-pressure upon Parliament made obstruction possible? If the House of Commons had enough time and to spare for the transaction of all its business, the art could not be practised with success. It was the fact that the House was overworked that suggested to a minority the possibility of defeating measures by a systematic prolongation of business. Obstruction is not the cause of the disease; it is only a fresh development of it. To treat it as the original complaint is the result of a mistaken diagnosis, and the event has proved that none of the drastic remedies which have been devised for the purpose of putting down obstruction have proved successful. Our attention has merely been diverted from the real source of the evil.

Let us, therefore, probe a little deeper into the question, and endeavour to define more precisely the source of the pressure which has produced this partial paralysis of Parliament. In order to do so, it is necessary to keep clearly in mind the functions which Parliament has to discharge.

CHAPTER II

THE FUNCTIONS OF PARLIAMENT

Few people realise the variety of the interests which Parliament controls, or the immensity of the legislative machine which has been developed out of the English Parliament in less than two hundred years. I say advisedly that it has been developed out of the English Parliament, because, although we talk of the union with Scotland and with Ireland, there was no union of Parliaments.[1] The Scotch and Irish Parliaments were destroyed, and Scotland and Ireland were permitted to send representatives to sit in the English House of Lords and House of Commons. In neither case was there any reduction in the number of English representatives or of English peers. The English Parliament retained its ancient constitution; it merely absorbed into itself small additions of representation from Scotch and Irish constituencies, and from the Scotch and Irish peerages.

But although the sovereignty of the English

---

[1] The contrary can only be asserted in a highly technical sense. See Dicey's "England's Case against Home Rule," p. 244. No doubt in theory two sovereign bodies surrendered their sovereignty to a third sovereign body, but the facts are as stated in the text.

Parliament was thus imposed upon these two nations, it was not possible to impose the laws of England upon them in the same way. Before the unions were effected each State had reached that stage of social development which results in a highly complicated code of laws, and each of them had evolved a code which bore but little resemblance to those of the others. The differences between English and Scotch law were more numerous than those between English and Irish law, because Irish legislation had been under the control of the English Government, whereas Scotch law was a purely national evolution. So strong and deep is the demarcation between the systems of law in each of the three countries that, after nearly two hundred years of union with Scotland and nearly a hundred years of union with Ireland, there has been but a slight approach to amalgamation. If an attempt were made to codify the laws which are of common application to the three nations, it would be found necessary to omit nearly the whole of the laws relating to land, the church, the administration of justice, education, and local government, and also a considerable portion of the law relating to trade.[1] Such a code would be found to consist almost entirely of laws relating to the raising and expenditure of revenue, the maintenance and control of the army and the navy, and of laws

---

[1] See *post*, p. 311.

for improving the great administrative departments of the Government.

So it will be seen that the English Parliament, when it effected the unions, took upon itself a very serious load of responsibility. It placed the Scotch and Irish representatives in an absolute and hopeless minority in the United Parliament, and it undertook the duty of legislating for each of the three nations separately upon all those questions which most closely touch their social life and well-being.

But these delicate and complicated duties by no means exhaust the claims which are made upon the time and attention of Parliament. We are too apt to forget the immense extent of our political responsibilities. No sovereign legislature ever attempted to bear so overwhelming a burden. Scattered all over the earth's surface we find political communities which are dependent to a greater or less extent upon the efficiency of our parliamentary machine. These communities divide themselves into two categories. There are, first, those which possess a local autonomy which is dependent upon our sovereign government, either by toleration, as in the case of the Isle of Man and the Channel Islands, or by direct creation, as in the case of the great self-governing colonies; and second, those colonies and dependencies which have no local autonomy, whose affairs are administered by the Government of the United Kingdom, either directly or by delegation. Foremost among these is India, a continent in itself, inhabited by more than 200,000,000 people, various in race, language and creed. Besides that portion which is directly under British sway, there are about 200 important dependent States under native rulers whose political relations must needs be regulated by the Indian Government: a congeries of nations for whose welfare we have made ourselves responsible.

Now we must note particularly that this enormous expansion of power and responsibility has to a very great extent taken place since 1800. The Indian Empire was indeed the creation of the last century, but its consolidation and the assumption of direct responsibility for it is the work of the present. The foundation of that vast aggregation of States in South Africa, where we have lately been adding Crown colony to Crown colony with as much rapidity as an energetic farmer might show in the enclosure of waste land for cultivation, dates from 1806. When the first Parliament of the United Kingdom met, Australia was inhabited by cannibals, kangaroos and convicts; Tasmania and New Zealand were unoccupied by Europeans.

These facts illustrate the vast expansion which has been taking place during the present century. The new problems which have been necessarily raised by that expansion are not only complex but also of supreme importance. Take as an example one of these problems. By our continuous annexations in Africa, our political relations with certain European powers have been entirely changed. We have now Crown colonies whose frontiers march with those of the colonial possessions of France, Germany and Portugal. We are no longer a power whose possessions can only be attacked by these nations from seaward.[1] Their armies have but to step across an imaginary line to invade our territory.

Consider, then, how greatly the work of Parliament has been increased, or if Parliament has been efficient, it ought to have been increased, by these mighty changes. Not only do all these dependencies, even those which have been granted self-government, require legislation at the hands of the Imperial Parliament, but their mutual and external relations demand vigilant supervision. When a question of colonial confederation arises, Parliament must pronounce the final decision upon it; when Newfoundland goes bankrupt and corrupt, Parliament has to look into the matter; when a French patrol enters a "British sphere of influence," the mightiest consequences of peace or war may depend upon the effect of a few words uttered in the House of Commons.

[1] Canada is an exception to the foregoing remarks; but even in regard to Canada the frontier difficulty is practically the growth of the present century.

Members of the House must therefore understand these questions if our system of government is to be efficient. They must understand them because at any moment the fate of a ministry may depend upon a vote taken on any one of them. And they can only be understood after full and deliberate investigation and discussion. We ought to find, therefore, that debates in the House of Commons upon foreign and colonial questions have very largely increased during recent years. Whether that has been the case we shall see later on.[1]

We have now taken a bird's-eye view of the duties and responsibilities of Parliament. It must be admitted that they are both many and onerous, and that the burden of them is likely to increase year by year. We have seen that Parliament has to safeguard the interests of the three kingdoms where they are identical, and also to regulate those interests of the three kingdoms which are separate. It has to consider and decide upon an amazing number of foreign and colonial questions which involve considerations of the most vital and pressing importance. The task is indeed Herculean.

Let us now turn our attention to another aspect of the problem. Let us leave the consideration of what Parliament ought to do, and look at what it is actually doing.

[1] See *post*, p. 77.

I will suppose that the reader is an elector in an English constituency, and that the member for his division came down to address his constituents upon the work of the first session of 1895. What was the burden of that member's speech? He probably commenced with a lamentation over the amount of work demanded of Parliament, and he explained the absolute impossibility of carrying all the bills which had been brought forward by Government during the session. Then he proceeded to deal with the measures which had most occupied the attention of Parliament. He discoursed upon the high moral principle, or the barefaced robbery, involved in the Bill for the Disestablishment of the Church in Wales; he praised or blamed the policy which underlies the Scotch Crofters' Bill and the Irish Land Bill; he discussed the merits of the Local Veto Bill, and whether it was prudent to confine its operation to Great Britain; and he perhaps referred to the Factory Act, and to the question of electoral reform which is popularly known as "One man, one vote." If time served, he possibly concluded with a passing allusion to the Indian cotton duties.

Now I can conceive that my reader might return home after hearing such a speech to make some curious reflections. "This is surely a very extraordinary business," he might say. "This United Parliament of a United Kingdom seems to have marvellous little unity about it. Only two measures, and one of them merely a small question of electoral reform, out of all those about which our member has discoursed so eloquently, are intended to apply to all the three kingdoms. Of the rest, Ireland is clamouring for one, Scotland for a second, and Wales for a third. And what seems more remarkable, Irish members are voting for the Welsh Disestablishment Bill, with which their constituents have no concern whatever, because they want to secure the passing of their own Land Bill; and the Scotch members are threatening that they won't vote for the Welsh Disestablishment Bill, with which their constituents have no concern, not for that chivalrous reason, but because they want to force the progress of their Crofters' Bill, which, they fear, is going to be squeezed to death. And, most remarkable of all, this Local Veto Bill, which, if it be good in principle, is surely good for all the three kingdoms, is limited to England and Scotland, because the Irish members will support it only on the condition that its provisions are not extended to constituencies which they represent. Moreover, it seems probable that many of these measures, after all the turmoil, will never be considered fully. And, beyond that passing reference to India, so far as I can see, Parliament has no time to cast even a hasty glance at colonial questions. The business of Parliament seems an incomprehensible muddle!"

The object of the following pages is to elucidate the causes of these objections, and to prove that the disadvantages which they illustrate are permanent, not temporary, in their character. It will be shown, by an analytical examination of its work, that Parliament is actually suffering from over-pressure, which has produced a partial paralysis of its functions; and an attempt will be made to fix approximately the date at which that over-pressure commenced. The causes of the over-pressure will then be examined, and it will be proved that it is, to a great extent, due to the increasing demands made by England, Scotland and Ireland for separate attention, and more especially to the needs of England. It will be shown, further, not only that the interests of each country have suffered on account of this over-pressure, but also that those vast joint and imperial interests which are involved in foreign relations and colonial affairs have been perforce neglected.

This will form the foundation of fact upon which the superstructure of argument will be raised. It will be at once perceived that, if the foundation can be made good, the argument must necessarily be that the policy of the Acts of Union of 1707 and 1800, however wise it may have been at those dates, has, in changed circumstances, broken down, and that our present "unitarian" constitution is injurious, not only to the several portions of the United Kingdom, but to their joint interests. I shall endeavour to show that this is the case; and, further, that the policy of the unions has now resulted in the destruction of certain constitutional doctrines, which are supposed to form the basis not only of our own constitution, but of all free democracies, and that it has entailed certain evils which, if they are permitted to flourish unchecked, may ultimately sap the life of democratic government.

These considerations will complete the first section of this inquiry. In the second section the subject will be dealt with from the historical standpoint. The conditions which have prevented identity of interests between the three countries will be investigated, and the question whether those conditions are being modified in the direction of greater union or further separation will be examined. It will be necessary also to consider the causes which led to the incorporating unions; whether they were the transient exigencies of the moment, or the permanent needs of the uniting States. And, lastly, an endeavour will be made to discover whether each of the three countries is conscious of the disadvantages of the existing system, and, if so, by what means it is attempting to escape from them.

To sum up, I shall attempt to establish the following propositions, namely:—

1. That Parliament, through over-pressure of business, is incapable of transacting efficiently the work demanded of it.

2. That this over-pressure results from the increasing demands for separate attention by the three countries included in the incorporating union.

3. That these separate demands tend to increase, to the injury not only of each nation, but also of imperial interests.

4. That the present system tends to weaken constitutional government.

5. That each of the three nations is conscious, in a greater or less degree, of the disadvantage entailed upon it, and is seeking to escape from the results of that disadvantage.

6. That the causes which brought about the incorporating unions were due to mere transient necessity, and not to the permanent requirements of the incorporating States.

If these propositions can be made good, I shall claim to have proved that the relations of the three component portions of the United Kingdom are such as to demand a federal rather than an incorporating union; that we are, in fact, endeavouring to conduct a federal government under the guise of unity. The last section will therefore be devoted to the consideration of the various objections to any system of federal government, both in the abstract and as applied to our own constitution, and to an inquiry whether it may not be possible to effect a reform which, while avoiding those disadvantages that may be demonstrated to exist in federal government as it is generally understood, may remedy the proved evils of our existing system with the least possible amount of friction and dislocation.

II

THE FOUNDATIONS

CHAPTER III

THE METHODS OF INVESTIGATION

Before proceeding to investigate the causes which have brought about the parliamentary paralysis which has been asserted to exist, it is necessary to call attention to a proposition which, if valid, would render a large part of the inquiry superfluous. Professor Dicey, in the introductory chapter of a book entitled "A Leap in the Dark," makes the following statement. "Every member of Parliament has always stood upon a footing of perfect equality with his fellows; the representatives of a county or of a borough, English members, Scotch members, Irish members, have hitherto possessed precisely equal rights, and have been subject to precisely the same duties. They have been sent to Parliament by different places, but, when in Parliament, they have not been the delegates of special localities, they have not been English members, or Scotch members, or Irish members, they have been simply members of Parliament; their acknowledged duty has been to consult for the interest of the whole nation; it has not been their duty to safeguard the interests of particular localities or countries."[1]

Now if members of Parliament could be persuaded of the reasonableness of this contention; if Scotch members could be convinced that it was no part of their duty to promote the Crofters' Bill, and if Irish members would recognise that they were acting in a highly unconstitutional manner when they press the claims of the Irish Land Bill, much of the difficulty would disappear. The necessity for separate legislation for the three countries is, as will be proved, one of the prime causes of parliamentary paralysis. If there were no special force pressing such legislation forward, much of it would never take its place in the statute book, and the parliamentary congestion would be at once relieved. But the question remains: Is it in the nature of things possible, and if so is it desirable, that such a conviction should be brought home to the consciences of members? While examining into the causes of parliamentary paralysis we must also consider whether it is reasonable to contend that it is the "acknowledged duty" of members of the House of Commons "to consult for the interest of the whole nation," and not "to safeguard the interests of particular countries."

It is not possible to make the investigation interesting. It deals with very dull statistics,

[1] "A Leap in the Dark," p. 7.

from which, it is to be feared, most people will turn away in despair. But I believe that these statistics take us down to the root of our present difficulty, and that they enable us to test the accuracy of professorial speculation by ascertained fact.

It has already been said that our constitution is living, developing, constantly adapting itself to new requirements and to changed conditions. In many cases this development is gradual, hardly to be observed, like the growth of a plant; in others it is only effected after struggle, as a snake casts his skin. The former development results in what is called the custom of the constitution, and may be illustrated by the lapse of the royal prerogative to dismiss ministers at pleasure, to which reference has already been made. The latter development forms the law of the constitution, and can result only from the deliberate decision of the legislature, embodied in an Act of Parliament. The two Acts of Union and the various Reform Acts are types of this class of development.

Now if it be the "acknowledged duty" of members of the House of Commons "to consult for the interest of the whole nation," and not "to safeguard the interests of particular countries," that duty must be the result of constitutional custom. It does not depend upon statute. But constitutional custom originates in a practice which, on account of its convenience, gradually becomes habitual. If the circumstances change and the practice becomes no longer convenient, we must expect to find an alteration in the custom.

But parliamentary congestion, if we are right in assuming that it is not merely due to the practice of obstruction, is probably the result of defective parliamentary mechanism which is dependent upon constitutional law. If this be so, we shall not necessarily find any tendency towards silent and gradual repair. The fault can only be remedied by legislation, which involves conflict and delay; but until it is remedied we must expect to find that the evil grows gradually worse.

Thus we have two issues before us, but the determination of them depends upon the same evidence. They must of necessity be considered together, but it is important that we should keep them separate and distinct in our minds.

With regard to the former, it may be at once admitted that, before the union with Scotland, it was "the acknowledged duty" of members "to consult for the interests of the whole nation." This was because the Parliament of England legislated for England alone, except in the very rare cases in which it interfered as lord paramount in Ireland. An English member concerned himself with English affairs for the simple reason that, practically, there were no other affairs with which he was able to concern himself. The doctrine that, when he was elected, he represented, not his constituency, but the whole nation, was therefore intelligible. He was not called upon to deal with questions, other than purely local and personal questions, which did not affect the nation at large.

But when the union with Scotland was effected, the conditions were entirely changed. If a Scotch member had been told in 1708 that it was not his duty to safeguard the interests of his particular country, it would have amazed him considerably. "My business here," he would have said, "is to safeguard the interests of Scotland under the Act of Union, interests which you English seem mightily inclined to infringe. My business also is to get Acts passed for the benefit of Scotland, which two years ago we should have obtained from our own Parliament, and it is likely that I shall have a hard task of it." The constitutional custom of the English Parliament would seem mere foolishness to this Scotchman. The circumstances in which that custom grew up had changed.

The change was accentuated when, nearly a hundred years later, the Irish contingent was introduced into the Parliament of Great Britain. New questions were thus brought within the scope of parliamentary control which affected Ireland, and Ireland only, in regard to which

Scotch and English members represented no interest whatever. It would appear manifest to Irish members that their prime duty was to safeguard the interests of Ireland, and all other considerations would be subordinated to the performance of that duty.

But it is contended that the English, Scotch and Irish members, so far as they have been employed in safeguarding the interests of their own particular countries, have been acting in an unconstitutional manner, that is to say that they have broken down the ancient constitutional custom of the English Parliament. The question is, could they have acted otherwise; and the answer depends upon the proportion which the separate transactions for each nation bear to the total transactions of Parliament. If those separate transactions are proportionately small, the question becomes insignificant; the larger they turn out to be, the more complete is the proof of the necessity for breaking down or reforming the traditional custom of the English Parliament.

The work of Parliament divides itself into two great branches. The first is the work of legislation, the second is the work of controlling by its votes the administrative action of the Government. The work in each branch is susceptible of analysis. We can determine how many Acts of Parliament, passed in any one year, apply to the whole of the United Kingdom, and how many affect only the interests of its component parts. We can also determine, by the help of "Hansard," with less rigid but nevertheless approximate accuracy, how many debates took place which were conducted for some purpose other than the direct promotion of legislation, and what proportion of them related to the United Kingdom and to each component State. These two analyses will furnish the information which we seek; the solid basis of fact upon which conclusions may be founded with safety, instead of the shifting sand of speculation and of theory.

If we wish to conduct our observations with absolute accuracy, we must bring as long a period as possible under focus. It is useless to record the results of one, two, or three years only, because it might chance that they would be contradicted if other years had been selected. I propose, therefore, in order to consider the subject as exhaustively as possible, to submit an analysis of legislation between 1707 and 1800, and also between 1801 and 1890; and an analysis of debates for the latter period, that is, for the nine complete decades which have elapsed since the union with Ireland.

But the figures for each year would be bewildering, and would also, perhaps, mislead. To submit them in the form of annual results would be open to the manifest objection that one Act, one debate, may in time value be equal to thirty other Acts or debates. To obviate this difficulty, the decade, not the year, has been made the time unit. The legislation and discussions for each decade have been averaged. By this method the great and the small are reduced to one common measure of value.

The question of legislation will be dealt with first. To afford a basis for comparison, it is necessary to estimate the legislative capacity of the English and Scotch Parliaments respectively before the Union. For this purpose it is useless to go back further than 1688, the date at which, in England, annual Parliaments and government upon modern constitutional principles commenced. The period will be divided, as nearly as possible, into two decades, and the work of the decades will be averaged. The earlier average is for nine years only. From 1688 to 1696 the average number of public general statutes passed by the English Parliament annually was 24·5 ; and for the following decade the average was 26·5. During the same period the Scotch Parliament did not hold annual sessions, but it may be assumed that it succeeded in transacting all necessary business, and its results may therefore be averaged in the same manner. But a comparison of its work with that of the English Parliament cannot be made upon the basis of the total number of Acts passed, because the Scotch statutes were not classified, like the English, into "public general" and "private" Acts. If the gross total of Scotch legislation were dealt with, it would show an average of 60·2 Acts for the period 1688-1696, and of 28·7 Acts for the remaining decade. These figures are evidently misleading. An analysis has therefore been made of the Scotch legislation for the period in question, separating from the gross total those Acts which, according to the then current English classification, would have been termed "public general" statutes. This analysis shows the figures to stand thus: for the period 1688-1696, the average was 16·6 per annum; and for the remaining period it was 5·9 per annum. The decrease is startling; it may probably be partly accounted for by the violence of the opposition to the Act of Union, which may have tended to hinder other legislation.

Now one of the questions which might have occurred to the commissioners for the union of the two countries was whether, granting that it was expedient that an Imperial Parliament should legislate, not only for the joint, but also for the several needs of the united realms, the time at the disposal of such a Parliament would be sufficient for the purpose. The question was one which was capable of receiving a very definite answer. Even if there should be no reduction in the total legislation by dealing in one Act with joint questions, there was no reason to doubt that the proposed Parliament of Great Britain would have plenty of time for its work. The total average of statutes for the two kingdoms for 1688 - 1696 was 41·1, and for the remaining period 32·4. Both Parliaments had recently, on more than one occasion, passed a larger number of Acts than the former average in one session. No reasonable man could imagine that, having regard to the probable amount of the legislative business which the united Parliament would have to transact, there could be any objection to the proposed scheme for union on the ground that the time at the disposal of Parliament would be insufficient for the performance of its legislative functions. Whether Scotland would benefit by the delegation of its separate legislation to a Parliament in which a vast majority knew nothing of, and cared little for, its local needs, was a different question, and one upon which men at that time could only speculate.

The figures quoted above enable us to form an estimate of the amount of legislative work which the English Parliament transacted, and also an approximate estimate of the additional legislative labours which would be imposed upon it by the absorption of the work of the Scotch

Parliament. It is now necessary to consider the course of legislation in the Parliament of Great Britain from its commencement to the date of the Act of Union with Ireland. This may be stated at once in a tabular form. The averages are for decades in every case except the last, which is for four years.

Date.	Federal.*	States.				Total States.	Total Legisln.
		England.	Scotland.	Ireland.	Colonies.		
1707-16	16·0	12·3	2·2	·5	·3	15·3	31·3
1717-26	11·7	14·8	2·5	·3	·2	17·8	29·5
1727-36	12·9	18·4	1·6	·3	·9	21·2	34·1
1737-46	13·9	22·1	2·0	—	·7	24·8	38·7
1747-56	16·0	40·4	3·6	·1	·9	45·0	61·0
1757-66	22·5	52·8	2·9	·2	2·3	58·2	80·7
1767-76	27·5	62·1	5·1	·4	2·9	70·5	98·0
1777-86	44·5	60·0	4·2	1·0	2·2	67·4	111·9
1787-96	45·2	80·6	8·8	·1	3·1	92·6	137·8
1797-1800	81·0	90·5	17·5	—	6·0	114·0	195·0

* In the following pages the word "federal" has been employed to denote legislation which affected the whole of Great Britain, or, subsequent to 1801, of the United Kingdom, or of the Empire. "States" legislation denotes legislation affecting certain portions only.

The accompanying diagram records the results of the foregoing figures. The upright columns represent decades, except the last, which represents a period of four years only.

Each of the transverse sections represents an aggregate of ten statutes. The erratic lines crossing the squares so formed represent the

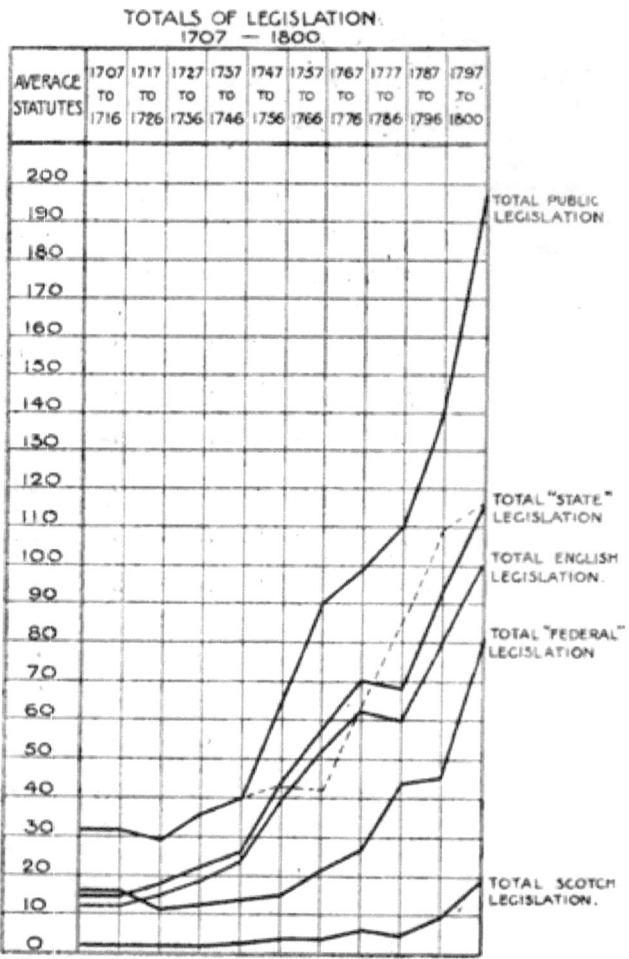

growth or diminution of the various classes of legislation for each decade.

This diagram requires a few words of explanation. For forty-five years after the Act of Union, the old English classification of statutes into "public general" and "private" Acts was adopted. But the growth of Acts of a purely local character was so enormous that in 1752 the titles only of most of these Acts were printed in the Statute-book. This arrangement was continued until 1798. In that year the local Acts were entitled, "publick local and personal Acts," and they were numbered separately for citation. In order to obtain an accurate idea of the legislative work of the century, it was essential that this arbitrary classification should be disregarded. All the Acts which would have been classed as "publick" at the date of the Union have been treated as public throughout the whole period. The dotted line which leaves the line of total legislation at the end of the fourth decade, represents the average of public general statutes which were printed after the re-classification of 1752. The "private" legislation, which also shows a remarkable increase, is not accounted for in the table. That class of legislation included all Acts for the enclosure of commons. Some idea of the enormous amount of work done by Parliament in this respect may be obtained from the fact that the average number of enclosure Acts passed annually during the decade ended with the year 1776 was 60·1. For some inexplicable reason, during the last four years of the period under review, a certain number of enclosure Acts were allowed to appear under the heading of " publick local and personal Acts." This variation from precedent would, if these Acts had been taken into account, have unduly exaggerated the growth of business during the last four years, which is startling enough as the figures stand. They have, therefore, been excluded from the computation.

The diagram exhibits the enormous growth of the legislative work of Parliament during the eighteenth century. The average for the last four years is six times the average for the first decade of the Union. The State legislation for England shows, except in one insignificant case, a uniform, and latterly a rapid increase ; but an increase which is mainly due to local needs. These local Acts may be classified under three heads : (1) for the making and repair of roads ; (2) for improving harbours, navigable rivers and canals ; and (3) for conferring local government upon towns. These, and the enclosure of commons and common fields were the prime objects of English legislation during the latter part of the eighteenth century. The enclosure Acts are lost sight of in the category of private Acts, but their effect for good or evil upon the future of England was probably as great as that of any class of Acts which finds a place in the Statute-book. If they were enumerated among the State laws affecting England, they would swell her share of legislation enormously.

The position of Scotland is worthy of especial consideration. The small proportion which its State legislation bears to that of England will no doubt cause astonishment.[1] The figures may at first sight appear to be evidence of the ease with which Scotland was absorbed into the Union. But such a conclusion cannot be accepted unhesitatingly. Questions relating to revenue, national defence, and the constitution, and, to a partial extent, questions relating to trade and offences, were practically the only subjects upon which Parliament could legislate federally. In regard to such questions as the administration of justice, the Church, land and local administration, the existing laws of Scotland so differed from those of England that it was impossible for Parliament to deal with them in that manner. The supposition that the State interests of Scotland were neglected for the sake of the State interests of the "predominant

[1] It must be remembered that the task of distinguishing between the statutes relating to Great Britain, England and Scotland respectively, during the earlier part of the eighteenth century, is one of extreme difficulty. The rational assumption would be that, unless otherwise declared in the statute itself, it applied to Great Britain. But this is in a large number of cases negatived by the scope of the statute. Where a statute, not limited to one of the countries by declaration, contains no machinery for enforcing it in Scotland, it has been classed as relating to England.

partner," is at least as plausible as the theory of easy amalgamation. Again, it will be noted that while the progress of State legislation for England is practically uniform, the progress of that for Scotland is erratic. But the causes which were operating to necessitate increased State legislation for England were equally active in Scotland. Scotland enjoyed free trade with England, and was upon a footing of equality with her in foreign and colonial trade. She profited equally with the sister country in the benefits accruing from the expansion of the Empire. The need for increased facilities for trade intercommunication and urban improvements—the characteristic work of the century —must have been felt by Scotland not less keenly than by England. Why then was not the progress uniform, and why was not the body of Scotch State legislation greater? The tempting answer is that a State, with special needs, which is represented by a small minority in a Parliament, will obtain, not all the legislation which it requires, but so much as it can snatch. This, it will be shown, is inevitably the case when the time at the disposal of Parliament is insufficient for the transaction of its work. But there is no evidence in the figures that this straining-point had been reached during the eighteenth century. To avoid the use of any doubtful argument, it must be assumed that the small amount of State legislation which Scotland obtained was sufficient for her requirements. But it is manifest that the Parliament of Great Britain remained in essence the Parliament of England. The great bulk of its work was English work. Occasionally only had legislation to be undertaken for the benefit of the small appanage called Scotland.

But it may be urged that these figures and this diagram show only the rates of progress, not the proportions which the federal and State legislation bore to one another. In the following table the figures of the previous table are turned into percentages.

Date.	Federal.	States.				Total.
		England.	Scotland.	Ireland.	Colonies.	
1707-16	51·1	39·3	7·0	1·6	1·0	48·9
1717-26	39·6	50·1	8·4	1·0	·9	60·4
1727-36	37·8	53·9	4·6	·8	2·9	62·2
1737-46	35·9	57·1	5·2	—	1·8	64·1
1747-56	26·2	66·2	6·0	·2	1·4	73·8
1757-66	27·9	65·4	3·6	·2	2·9	72·1
1767-76	28·1	63·3	5·2	·4	3·0	71·9
1777-86	39·9	53·6	3·7	·9	1·9	60·1
1787-96	32·8	58·5	6·4	·1	2·2	67·2
1797-1800	41·6	46·4	8·9	—	3·1	58·4

A translation of these figures into diagram form gives the following result.

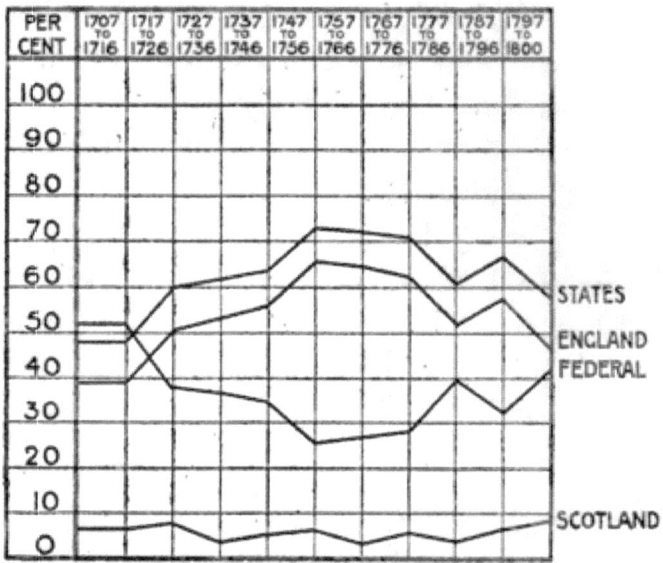

These figures do not appear in any way to negative the conclusions which have been deduced from the earlier table, although in some respects they modify them. The pre-eminence of England is fully maintained, and it is interesting to note that the line of English legislation runs almost exactly parallel to the line of total State legislation. The space between the two lines represents the amount of States legislation devoted to Scotland, Ireland and the Colonies. It is curious to observe how nearly equal is that amount in each decade. This confirms the supposition that England insisted upon what may be termed a "first call" upon the time at the disposal of Parliament for purposes of States legislation, but it affords no conclusive evidence that the remaining time was insufficient to meet the legitimate needs of the remaining States. But the diagram reveals the fact that apparent individual progress is by no means the same thing as actual relative progress. The periods during which the States legislation is apparently making its greatest leaps, namely, the sixth and seventh decades and the last four years, were, relatively, periods of decline. One fact is clear: the proportion of States legislation increased, and the proportion of federal legislation declined, until the middle of the century. From that time the disproportion was gradually but fluctuatingly reduced; but at the end of the period the percentage of State legislation was larger and the percentage of federal legislation was smaller than they had been during the first decade of the Union. A more minute analysis shows that the relative increase in federal legislation which produced the relative decrease in State legislation was due almost entirely to an increase of legislation under three heads, namely, Revenue, National Defence and Trade. And the greater part of this trade legislation was "war" legislation; duties, bounties and prohibitions having been used as weapons of offence and defence in the great struggle with France, which was then being carried on. It was due to the exigencies of the moment, not to the gradual welding of permanent interests between the two States of England and Scotland. If the annual finance legislation could have been effected, as at present, by four or five Acts, and if there had been no war of tariffs, the federal legislation would have shown no relative increase.

It will be noticed that in this and the following chapter no mention is made of Welsh legislation. The reason is that the amount of separate legislation for the Principality has been so small that it was not worth recording. The laws of England and Wales are practically identical. On the basis of legislation no case can be made out for the separate treatment of the latter. The terms " Great Britain " and " England " in this investigation must be understood as including " Wales."

CHAPTER IV

THE LIMIT OF LEGISLATIVE CAPACITY

THE course of legislation during the eighteenth century shows us that the question, which could scarcely have occurred to the commissioners for the Union between England and Scotland, namely, whether the united Parliament would be capable of transacting the whole of the work of the united kingdoms, ought to have presented itself for consideration to the framers of the Union of Great Britain and Ireland.

During the interval the work of Parliament had increased six-fold, and while that Union was being negotiated it was increasing with far greater rapidity than ever before. But a consideration of the subject-matter of current legislation would modify the weight of this argument very considerably. The question would probably present itself to the average member of Parliament at that time somewhat in this fashion. "It is true," he might argue, "that just for the present we are terribly pressed with business, but the war can't go on indefinitely; we must smash France soon, and then we shall get relief from this eternal succession of money bills and other war legislation. And beyond that, of what does our work mainly consist? Why, of road-making, improving harbours and rivers, cutting canals, giving towns power to clean and light themselves, and enclosing commons. But that kind of work cannot last for ever. The roads are already nearly completed, and our system of waterway, so essential to our commercial prosperity, is well advanced. There are few towns which are not now decently paved, and lighted with oil lamps, at any rate on 'dark' nights; and as for the commons, there is a limit even to them. In a short time they will all be enclosed. It really looks as if in the near future Parliament would have very little to do. Why not, therefore, take over this miserable Irish business and try to settle it? If she gives us no more legislative work than Scotland has given us—and why should she?—we shall have no difficulty in managing it."

Now what was the legislative work for Ireland which it was proposed that the united Parliament should take over? The average legislation of the Irish Parliament during the last two decades of its existence—a period which is practically equivalent to the duration of the free Irish Parliament under the concessions of 1782—was as follows: 1781-1790, an average of 44·9 statutes per annum; and 1791-1800, an average of 55·9 statutes per annum. In two respects the case of Ireland differed from that of Scotland: first, the annual average of legislation was increasing, not diminishing; secondly, the terms of the proposed Union did not, as in the case of Scotland, contemplate the fusion of administrative departments. Even the Exchequers were at first kept separate. It could not be supposed, therefore, that any considerable part of the separate legislation which had, before the date of the Union, been necessary for Ireland would be effected by federal statutes, and it is clear that the risk of congestion and consequent paralysis of the legislative machine was by no means inconsiderable.

Let us now consider the legislative results of the constitution of 1800, from its birth to the end of the ninth decade of its existence, in the same manner as the work of the British Parliament has been considered. Before submitting the figures, it is necessary to repeat that, in order to secure a uniform basis of comparison during the eighteenth century, the sub-classification of statutes in 1752 into "publick," and "local and personal" was ignored. But the present comparison is quite independent of the former, and the analysis will be confined to "public general" statutes only. It must be borne in mind, however, that behind the body of legislative work which is dealt with, lies the large and (from 1840 onwards) the increasing class of local and personal statutes as well as the decreasing class of private Acts.

But during the period in question, a further re-classification was effected. Towards the middle of the century the practice of conferring quasi-legislative functions by Act of Parliament upon administrative departments and legally constituted corporate bodies came into vogue. These departments or bodies were empowered to make " provisional orders," and those orders were confirmed by Act of Parliament. Parliament, in fact, devolved upon others the right to settle the details of certain classes of legislation, retaining as it were a " right of veto," by insisting that legislation so proposed should pass through all the stages of a bill. The system was first adopted in the forties, and it became a common expedient in the two following decades. At first the Acts confirming provisional orders were classed among the public general statutes, but in 1868 they had become so numerous that they were relegated to the category of local and personal Acts. But to mark the distinction between them and the ordinary Acts of that class, their titles were set out immediately after the public general statutes under a separate heading.[1] But in process of time, other classes of Acts, not confirming provisional orders, which had previously been included among the public

[1] " The Acts contained in the following list, being public Acts of a local and personal character, are placed among the local and personal Acts."

general Acts, were relegated to this sub-class. To secure a common basis of comparison, these quasi-public general Acts have been included in the following table.

Date.	Federal.	States.								Total.
		Great Britain.	England and Ireland.	England.	Scotland.	Ireland.	Man.	Colonies.	Total.	
1801-10	25·9	40·9		23·0	4·8	31·9	·5	4·6	106·3	132·2
1811-20	39·8	35·8	1·2	29·3	4·9	31·7	·2	5·8	108·9	148·7
1821-30	34·4	7·0	1·2	25·2	6·3	19·5	·3	4·7	64·2	98·6
1831-40	34·7	3·6	1·5	34·0	6·6	17·9	·3	5·2	69·1	103·8
1841-50	36·0	4·0	4·2	34·8	5·3	23·0	·2	5·4	76·9	112·9
1851-60	35·4	3·9	2·7	43·6	9·4	17·3	·1	5·6	82·6	118·0
1861-70	41·7	4·6	3·2	41·1	11·6	19·0	·9	7·3	87·7	129·4
1871-80	34·5	1·6	2·8	41·7	9·8	19·1	·5	4·6	80·1	114·6
1881-90	29·0	1·0	3·6	57·7	9·2	18·4	·7	3·1	93·7	122·7

It will be noticed that in the first two decades the shares of Great Britain and of Ireland are abnormally large, and that in the third decade they are considerably reduced. This is due to the fact that the British and Irish Exchequers were not amalgamated until 1817. Before that year taxation had to be raised by separate Acts for Great Britain and for Ireland. The practice of the time was to impose taxation on each article, or small group of articles, by separate Acts. The period was one of war, involving very heavy taxation, and therefore the finance Acts were extremely numerous. This fact vitiates any generalisation that may be founded upon the figures relating to Ireland so far as these two decades are concerned. We do not reach the normal relations of the three countries until the decade 1821-1830.

In order to avoid a complication of lines, the foregoing table has been reduced to pictorial form in two diagrams. The first indicates (1) the course of total public general legislation; (2) that of the total States legislation; and (3) that of the total federal legislation.

The dotted line represents the course of legislation for Great Britain. The whole of that legislation is included in the total of States legislation, and the dotted line has been introduced only to show how profoundly the course of legislation was affected during the first two decades by the separation of the British and Irish Exchequers, and the consequent necessity for State, instead of "federal," finance legislation.

Two facts stand out clear and indisputable in this diagram. The first is that the average of "federal" legislation is small in comparison with the average of "States" legislation. If we further average the work of the last seven decades, we find that out of a total average of 114·3 statutes only 35·1 have been federal, while no less than

79.2 have related to States. That is to say, that less than a third of our legislation has been for the "united" kingdom. The second fact is that, small as is the average of federal legislation, it has, on the whole, decreased since

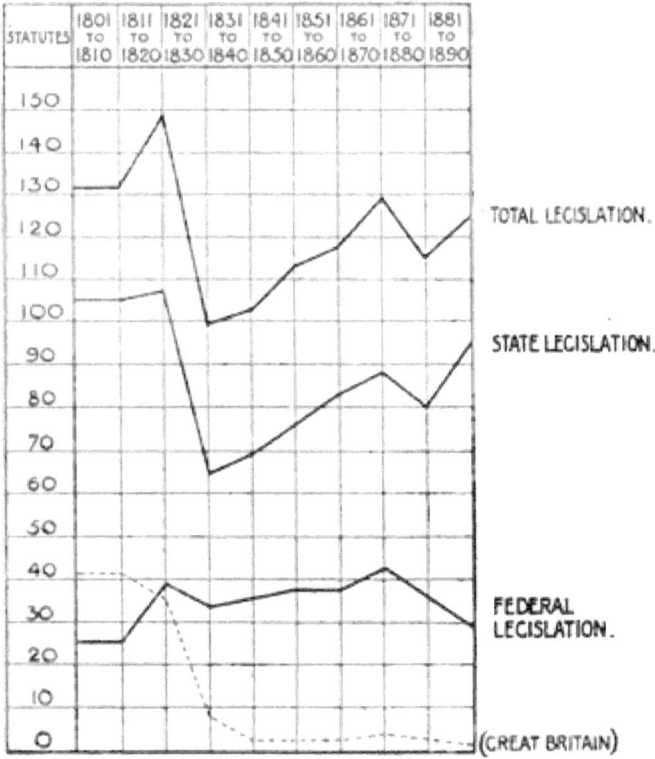

1820; while the average of States legislation has, on the whole, increased. Let us separate the figures of the third and the last decades from the rest, and look at them carefully:

	Federal.	States.	Total.
1821-30	34.4	64.2	98.6
1881-90	29.0	93.7	122.7

That is to say, in the third decade the federal legislation amounted to rather more than a third of the total; in the ninth it amounted to rather less than a fourth of it.

It is true that a certain proportion of the States legislation is local in character, and does not involve any national interest, but this does not affect the fact that, after the lapse of seventy years, the possibility of federal legislation has decreased. The Union of 1800 has not, therefore, made for unity in law.

Nor must it be supposed that when bills dealing with the same subject of legislation are brought into Parliament for each of the States separately, they are introduced in this form as a matter of convenience, and not from necessity. It cannot be imagined that any government would expose its policy to the dangers of two or three stormy passages through Parliament, when it could effect its purpose in one. A late Home Secretary, now Viscount Cross, has told us that a federal bill is always adopted in preference to States bills wherever that course is practicable. "I will never consent," he said, "so far as I can help it, to separate bills where one will do; but in many cases separate bills cannot be helped for the present."[1] Looking at the figures, it becomes a matter of curious speculation when that millennial period will arrive in which it will be possible to avoid "separate" bills.

[1] Hansard, vol. 232, c. 936.

One explanation of the reduction in federal legislation must, in fairness, be mentioned. The tendency has been to compress the total annual finance legislation (which is federal) into fewer and fewer Acts. The work which was done by eight or more Acts in the earlier part of the century is now effected by half a dozen or less. This tendency has reduced slightly the bulk of federal Acts, without a corresponding reduction in the federal work done. It is impossible to express this change in tabular form, but it would not have greatly affected the course of the lines on the diagram, if the old system of multiplicity of Acts had been maintained throughout the period.

Having thus ascertained that the tendency of legislation has been in favour of the States and to the disadvantage, or, at least, not in favour, of the United Kingdom, it is necessary to consider how the State legislation has been distributed. The diagram on the following page shows the position of England, Ireland and Scotland respectively.

The course of legislation for England and Scotland was not directly affected by the financial chaos of the first two decades. It will be seen that the share of England has largely increased. In 1881-90 it is more than double what it was in 1801-1810. The small share of Scotland has increased proportionately, but it has undergone a considerable diminution during the last two decades. The share of Ireland (from 1820) has practically remained stationary. The rapid rise during 1841-50 was due to legislation on account of the famine.

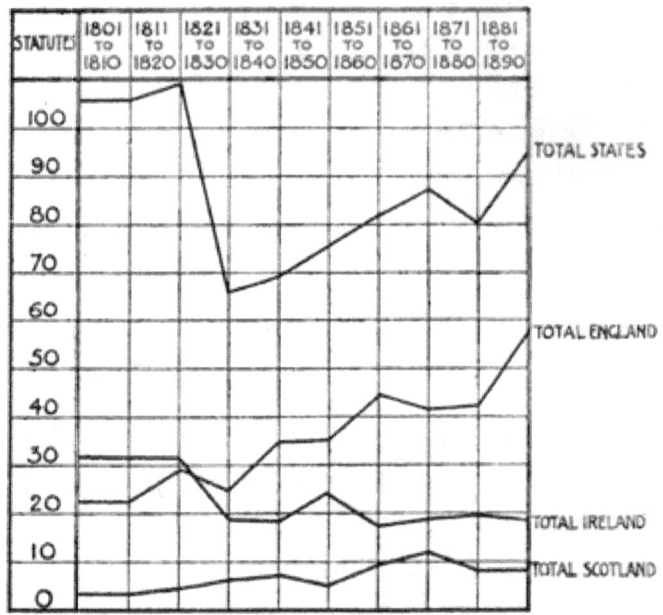

These facts give colour to the presumption that the Parliament of the United Kingdom has been, as the Parliament of Great Britain was, at heart and in fact the Parliament of England. Its work has been mainly, and is increasingly, English work. Its federal legislation has decreased; its Irish legislation has not increased; its Scotch legislation has increased only slightly, and has recently shown signs of decrease. The English interest only shows a definite expansion.

Let us now turn the table of averages into a table of percentages, and see what results are yielded.

Date.	Federal.	States.							Total.
		Great Britain.	England and Ireland.	England.	Scotland.	Ireland.	Man.	Colonies.	
1801-10	19·6	31·0	·4	17·4	3·7	24·1	·4	3·4	80·4
1811-20	26·8	23·5	·8	20·1	3·4	21·3	·1	4·0	73·2
1821-30	35·0	7·2	1·4	25·5	6·4	20·1	·3	4·1	65·0
1831-40	33·4	3·5	1·4	32·7	6·4	17·3	·3	5·0	66·6
1841-50	31·9	3·5	3·7	30·9	4·7	20·4	·2	4·7	68·1
1851-60	30·0	3·3	2·3	37·0	8·0	14·6	—	4·8	70·0
1861-70	32·2	3·7	2·5	31·8	8·9	14·6	·7	5·6	67·8
1871-80	30·1	1·4	2·4	36·4	8·6	16·7	·4	4·0	69·9
1881-90	23·7	·8	2·9	47·0	7·6	15·0	·5	2·5	76·3

The change does not affect the conclusions at which we have already arrived, but the figures show that the proportional decline of federal legislation since 1820 is greater than the average decline, and that the apparently stationary condition of Ireland was, relatively, retrogression. The percentages only serve to accentuate the fact that, so far as the legislative work of Parliament is concerned, State questions far outnumber federal questions, and that the disproportion is always growing.

With such a series of figures before us, we are able to estimate at its proper value the political dogma that it is the acknowledged duty of members of the House of Commons to consult for the interest of the whole nation, and not to safeguard the interests of particular localities or countries. The interests of the whole nation during the period 1821-1890 are represented by 30·7 per cent., and the interests of "particular localities or countries" by 69·3 per cent. of the total statutes passed. At the time when the doctrine of the "acknowledged duty" was formulated, no such conflict of interests prevailed: the Parliament of England legislated, with one or two unimportant exceptions, for the State of England only. The conditions which made such a doctrine possible have disappeared. We have introduced fresh conditions which have made it unworkable, and a new constitutional custom has sprung up. So long as more than two-thirds of our total legislation affects particular localities or countries, so long will it be the "acknowledged duty of," or, at any rate, there will be an imperative necessity for, members of the various nationalities to safeguard the interests of their "particular localities or countries." Whether the new doctrine is conducive to the interests either of the United Kingdom or each component State is a matter for future discussion. All that need be done at present is to prove that its genesis was inevitable; that it is founded on the bed-rock of political necessity.

The figures have thus conclusively disposed of one of the questions which has been raised. We see that, whether for good or evil, it has become inevitable that the members for the component States should safeguard the interests of those States. This is more especially the case with Scotland and Ireland, because the representatives of those countries are always in a minority in Parliament. It is less essential for England, who can always command a majority if she wishes it. Thus, although Irish and Scotch parties have been formed, no English party has yet been called into official existence. England has only lately begun an ominous grumble at the manner in which her State affairs are conducted.

Let us now see if the figures throw any light upon the causes of the congestion of Parliament. A glance at the table of percentages will show that the distinctively progressive section is the English section. If we add up the shares of all the other States we find that the totals decline proportionately to the increase of the English total. This increase of England's share in legislation may be quite natural and reasonable. That is not, at present, the question. All we have to do for the moment is to determine the source of the over-pressure upon Parliament; and, since we find that federal legislation is not increasing and that the percentage of States legislation, excluding

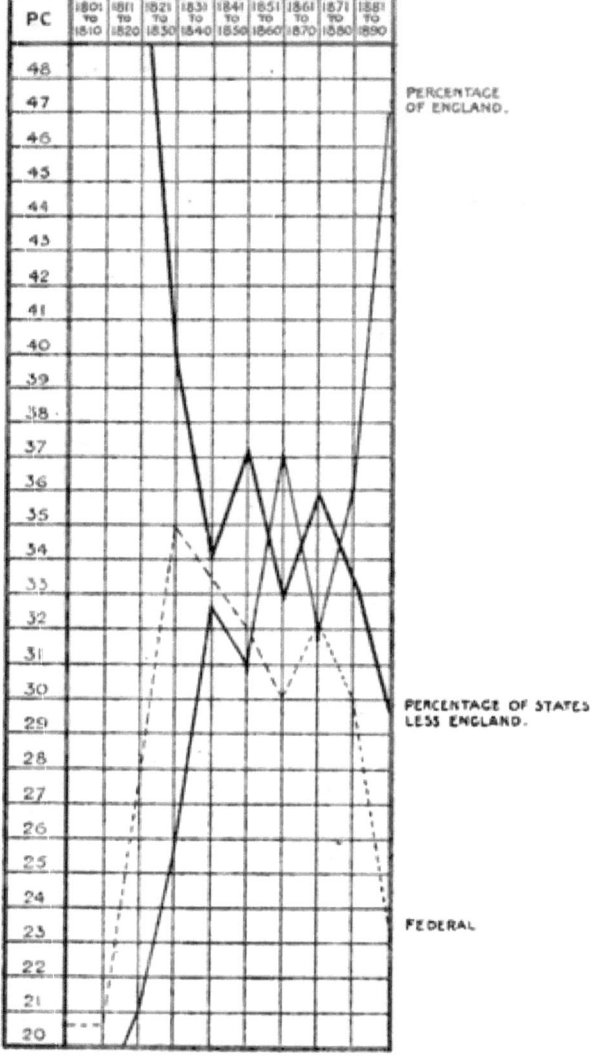

England, is rapidly diminishing, we are driven to the conclusion that the needs of England are the cause of the congestion.

The diagram on the preceding page gives the argument in pictorial form. The great proportionate increase of English legislation is remarkable. It must be remembered that we are dealing with percentages of figures which are themselves the averages of ten years' legislative work. We should expect to find the percentage of England large, but we should also expect to find the percentage of each State approximately uniform in each decade. If each State had succeeded in securing a fair proportion of legislative attention that result must have ensued. But instead of it we find the commander of the largest battalions annexing more and more of the common property. England recedes occasionally, but only to take a greater spring upwards. The other States make a slight recovery at times, but only to lose more ground in the end.

How, then, has it fared with the minor States, Scotland and Ireland? If we look at the percentages relating to these two countries since 1821 we notice this remarkable fact. In no case do they ever rise together. If the percentage for Ireland goes up, the percentage of Scotland goes down or remains stationary, and *vice versâ*. In the last decade both show a decline. If the shares of the two countries are added together it will be found that the totals in each decade vary only between a maximum of 26·5 per cent. and a minimum of 22·6 per cent., or a difference

of 4.0 per cent. only. Thus we discover that
the share of legislation accorded to Scotland and

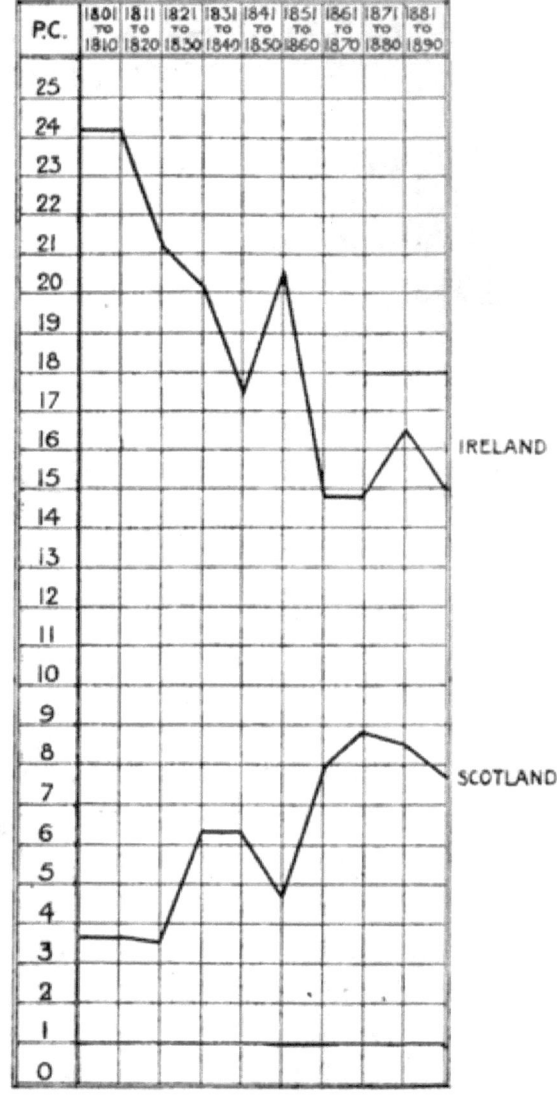

Ireland has in practice been limited to an average
of rather less than one-fourth of the total. And

the fact that these shares show a distinct tendency to vary inversely to one another, as exhibited in the diagram, proves that the allowance of legislation has been insufficient for the needs of the two countries, and that there has been a scramble going on between them to secure an adequate share.

It may be said then, that so far as Scotland and Ireland are concerned, there has always been congestion, that is, it has been impossible to compel Parliament to sit long enough to transact all Scotch and Irish business as well as all federal and English business. This will be found to be more emphatically true of Scotland than of Ireland, because Scotland has always had, numerically, the weakest representation. "Hansard" is full of complaints, made by Scotch members, that Scotch measures have been postponed, session after session, because there was no time to deal with them.

But this is not congestion from sheer inability to transact all the business which is brought before the House of Commons. It is congestion consequent upon neglect and the blandishments of an approaching 12th of August. It is a much more acute form of the disease from which Parliament is now suffering. If we are to discover its origin we must study the line of the legislation-absorbing factor, England.

Let us turn once again to the table of percentages, or the diagram on page 58, and observe the progress of English legislation in relation to the federal section. It will be noticed that, during the first five decades, with one insignificant exception, the ratio is direct. Where English legislation increases or decreases, federal legislation increases or decreases also. But after 1851 this condition is reversed. Instead of the ratio being direct, it is inverse. Where federal legislation is larger, England's share is reduced; where federal legislation is less, England's share leaps up. From 1850 onward, therefore, we find England's progress to be no longer in a direct line, but dependent upon the amount of federal legislation that has to be passed.

It must be remembered that this federal legislation includes all those Acts relating to national defence and finance, upon which our very existence as a nation depends. It also includes a large number of Acts effecting administrative reforms, which Cabinet Ministers have an interest in pushing forward. Everything must be sacrificed to the passing of the former class of bills. There is a considerable force behind the latter, driving them forward. When Parliament became incapable of transacting all the business demanded of it, it was inevitable that English progress should suffer a check, and should become dependent upon the nature and amount of the federal legislation which demanded the first attention.

It is reasonable to conclude, therefore, that, at some date subsequent to 1850, certainly within the decades 1850-70, a legislative time limit was reached ; that Parliament, having dealt with federal questions, which were, to a great extent, essential, had not at its disposal sufficient time to deal with all State legislation. The increase in English legislation, therefore, depended upon the relative decrease of federal legislation. If the number of federal Acts were small, the proportion of English Acts was augmented. If the federal needs increased, the share of England in legislation had to be diminished. Parliament became unable, from sheer pressure of work, to effect all the legislation which was demanded of it, and that result was chiefly due to the increased need for State as opposed to federal legislation. In other words, during the last forty years the presumption that an Imperial Parliament would be capable of transacting all the business of the States—a presumption which was indisputable at the date of the Union of Scotland with England, and which seemed plausible at the date of the Union with Ireland—has been disproved. The remodelling of the constitution, which was effected in 1800, has, from the point of view of legislative efficiency, broken down.

CHAPTER V

THE DEBATING FUNCTION

It will be well, before proceeding with this investigation, to take stock of the chief conclusions which have been drawn from the analysis of legislation which has occupied our attention. We have seen that a large and constantly increasing amount of parliamentary time and energy has been absorbed in legislating for the States individually, and that imperial, or, as it has been termed, "federal," legislation has been constantly decreasing in proportion. It has been demonstrated that the legislative share of England has increased to the detriment of the other two States; that Scotland and Ireland have been forced to compete against each other and against England for a rigorously limited amount of legislative attention; and, finally, that at some period subsequent to 1850, the limit of the capacity of Parliament for legislation had been reached, and that England herself had been compelled to submit to a curtailment of her demands.[1] But these conclusions are drawn

[1] See propositions 1, 2, and 3, p. 20.

from an analysis of the results of one function of Parliament only. The other, that of controlling the administration, and ventilating grievances by means of debate, which is a special function of the House of Commons, has not been taken into account. In order to render the inquiry exhaustive, it is necessary that this branch of the subject should be considered. But the difficulties in the way of making an analysis of it are far greater than they were in respect to the legislative work of Parliament. A statute is a statute, whether it consist of one or of two hundred and fifty sections. Personal judgment is not called upon to intervene in the decision of the question, and the method of averaging by decades reduces the great and the small to a common measure of value. A "debate" is not so sharply and conclusively defined. The line between a mere conversation, or a verbal skirmish, and a set debate cannot be rigidly drawn. Judgment must be exercised in the selection of those proceedings of Parliament which are to be reckoned as having attained to the dimensions of "debates," and with it is imported the possibility of error.

This difficulty is increased by the nature of the records upon which the analysis must of necessity be based. The reports of parliamentary proceedings since 1800 are upon an ascending scale of completeness. "Hansard" was not commenced until 1803, and the "Parliamentary Debates" which preceded it were fragmentary and meagre. And the earlier volumes of "Hansard" are by no means adequate records of what took place in Parliament. It is not until about 1830 that any great reliance can be placed upon the length of the reported speeches as evidence that a debate had taken place. In certain cases, during the earlier years, even the most curtailed reports are proved to be records of debates from internal evidence; but the possibility of error is greatly increased by the fact that this internal evidence had to be considered. It is increased also because, in dealing with a series of reports which become gradually more complete, the mental standard of what constitutes a "debate" has to be correspondingly raised. But this source of possible error only affects the earlier part of the analysis, and its averages. When those averages are turned into percentages, the error is in all probability eliminated, for it is reasonable to assume that the inadequacy of the reporting affected all classes of debate to the same extent, and that although the totals may result in an under-estimate, the ratios of each class to the others are not seriously affected.

A third difficulty arises from the necessity of defining precisely what debates should be included in the count. One of the objects of the inquiry is to estimate the effect of the debating function of the House of Commons in limiting the exercise of the legislative function. It is evident that all debates that take place during the normal course of a bill in its passage through the House must be absolutely excluded. It is no less evident that all debates upon motions and amendments which have no relation to a bill actually before the House must be brought into account.

These independent debates form by far the greater portion of those which have been enumerated. But between these two large classes, the position of which is indisputable, lies a group of debates of anomalous character. These are debates which can take place upon bills at certain stages, but which are originated or continued with the object of impeding rather than of facilitating their progress. A conspicuous example of this class of debates is that which arises upon an amendment to the motion for going into committee after the second reading of a bill has been carried. The object of such an amendment is nearly always obstructive. It raises a discussion which is of necessity germane to the subject of the bill, but which involves the consideration of some side issue. It is rarely successful, because the side issue has usually been dealt with in the debate upon the second reading. It is therefore practically an independent motion which tends to hinder

5—2

the House in the discharge of its legislative functions.

The same arguments apply, though perhaps less conclusively, to "instructions" to committees. An instruction is ostensibly a motion for improving the bill under discussion, but it is rarely used for that purpose; its object is almost invariably to impede, if not to destroy. Proof of this fact is afforded by the growing stringency of the Chair in ruling instructions out of order, and the growing ingenuity of opponents in the invention of instructions which, they hope, may succeed in passing the ordeal.

A still more doubtful class are the debates which arise upon motions for leave to bring in bills. The motion is one which is recognised in parliamentary procedure as a formal stage of legislation, but it is at the same time an absolutely superfluous stage. The text of the bill is not before the House; members gain their knowledge of its object and contents solely from the speech of the mover. Issues can be raised with which the proposed bill does not in any way deal, and the debate has more the character of a discussion upon a non-legislative subject than of one conducted for the professed furtherance of legislation.

All these three classes of anomalous debates have been included in the analysis. They all appear to constitute hindrances to the legislative function, which ought to be taken into account. But they have only been included after much hesitation ; and it might be reasonably contended that they would be more properly treated as debates in connection with the legislative function. Their exclusion, however, would not affect the results of the analysis to any appreciable extent. Their total is not large, and their average does not fluctuate greatly. They may tend to create an over-estimate of the averages of debates, but they do not affect the percentages.

The difficulties which beset the task which has been undertaken have been described with some minuteness because it is not pretended that the following figures represent more than a rough estimate. There is no possibility of such accuracy as was obtainable in the analysis of legislation. But they form, nevertheless, a fairly correct gauge of the growth of the debating function as a force competing against the legislative function in the absorption of the time of the House of Commons.

The table on the following page shows the averages of debates for the nine decades which have elapsed since 1800.

It must be noted that the United Kingdom has been credited with more than its legitimate share of debates. Its totals include all those discussions which could not be definitely allocated to any other class. But it must not be assumed that they were all "Federal" in their scope. The United Kingdom column includes all debates upon the custom and practice of Parliament. In it have been placed, for instance, discussions arising upon motions for the suspension of members, or adjournments

Date.	Federal.				States.				Total.
	United Kingdom.	Foreign.	Colonies.	Total.	England.	Ireland.	Scotland.	Total.	
1801-10	25·9	7·7	4·9	38·5	4·0	4·5	·3	8·8	47·3
1811-20	51·2	9·6	5·6	66·4	10·7	10·2	1·6	22·5	88·9
1821-30	49·1	6·1	9·5	64·7	15·9	14·4	2·1	32·4	97·1
1831-40	64·9	11·8	8·2	84·9	25·7	26·4	5·2	57·3	142·2
1841-50	61·4	13·2	12·0	86·6	28·7	21·2	3·0	52·9	139·5
1851-60	62·8	18·3	13·0	94·1	32·4	15·5	4·0	51·9	146·0
1861-70	54·8	17·3	10·0	82·1	33·5	19·2	4·7	57·4	139·5
1871-80	60·3	13·2	10·0	83·5	39·3	22·5	5·1	66·9	150·4
1881-90	53·6	11·2	5·6	70·4	27·3	37·5	8·7	73·5	143·9

for vacations, and also debates which related to Great Britain, in order to avoid opening a useless column. The object has been to enumerate in the "States" columns only such debates as related solely to the affairs of the particular State in question.

A separate column has been opened for debates

upon foreign affairs, for reasons which will appear hereafter. The colonial debates have been included in the "Federal" section, because, under any conceivable system of devolution, the control of the colonial department would remain with the Imperial Parliament.

The following diagram represents the relation

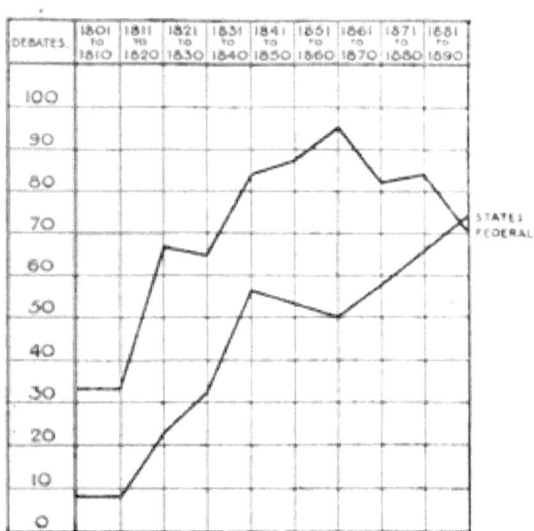

of the Federal and States averages given in the foregoing table.

It is apparent that, in spite of the undue inflation of the "Federal" total, which has been already explained, the debating power of Parliament has been more and more concentrated upon "States" questions. There was a decrease in the total of States discussions during the two decades 1841-60; a decrease which is accounted for entirely by the cessation of the pressure of Irish debates. Those decades include a period of lull in the story of Irish discontent, as it is told in the records of Parliament—a lull which was due, not to any diminution of that discontent, but to the fact that it was very meagrely represented in the House of Commons.[1] During those two decades there was a corresponding increase in the "Federal" debates; but subsequently the decrease under this head is considerable.

It will be noticed also that during the first four decades the increase of both classes of debates is almost continuous. From 1841 onwards, an increase or decrease in one class is accompanied by a corresponding decrease or increase of the other, with a very slight exception in the decade 1871-80. From that year therefore, the lines of the averages show, approximately, the same curves as they would assume if they were percentages. This fact will be apparent if this diagram be compared with the next, which shows the lines of the percentages. We have, in fact, an almost complete inverse pulsation between the lines of the averages of "Federal" and "States" debates since 1841, and the pulsation

---

[1] It is curious that the decade 1851-60, which followed immediately upon the period of Ireland's greatest disaster, should show the smallest percentage of Irish debates, except the decades before the Reform Acts.

is to the disadvantage of the "Federal" debates. This affords a sure indication that at some time since 1841, presumably between 1841 and 1860, the limit of parliamentary capacity for debate was reached, and increase in one class of discussion of necessity compelled a corresponding decrease in the other.

Date.	FEDERAL.				STATES.			
	United Kingdom.	Foreign.	Colonies.	Total.	England.	Ireland.	Scotland.	Total
1801-10	54·8	16·3	10·4	81·5	8·5	9·3	·7	18·5
1811-20	57·6	10·8	6·3	74·7	12·0	11·5	1·8	25·3
1821-30	50·5	6·3	9·8	66·6	16·3	14·9	2·2	33·4
1831-40	45·6	8·3	5·7	59·6	18·1	18·6	3·7	40·4
1841-50	44·0	9·5	8·6	62·1	20·6	15·2	2·1	37·9
1851-60	43·0	12·4	9·0	64·4	22·2	10·6	2·8	35·6
1861-70	39·3	12·3	7·2	58·8	24·0	13·8	3·4	41·2
1871-80	40·2	8·8	6·6	55·6	26·0	15·0	3·4	44·4
1881-90	37·2	7·8	3·9	48·9	19·0	26.1	6·0	51·1

The foregoing table is a reduction of the averages to percentages.

The lines of the percentages of "Federal" and "States" debates are depicted in the following diagram. It is inserted for the purpose of showing the correspondence in direction between the lines of the percentages and those of the averages since 1841.

Now the corresponding analysis of statutes which is contained in the preceding chapter showed that the limit of parliamentary capacity for legislation was reached at some period subsequent to 1850, presumably during the decades 1851-70. The present analysis indicates the

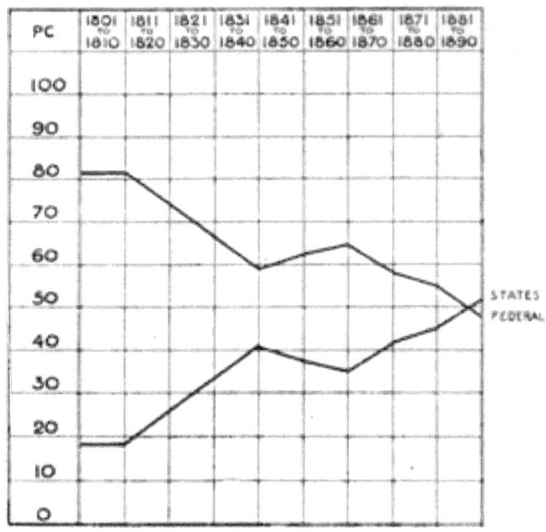

straining-point as commencing one decade earlier, and marks the decades 1841-60 as the period in which the limit of capacity was reached. The two periods overlap upon the decade 1851-60. In the previous decade the cup of parliamentary labour was rapidly filling; in the decade 1851-60 it overflowed. From that time onwards the House of Commons has been incapable of transacting all the work which has been demanded of it.

One main conclusion, therefore, which was deduced from the analysis of statutes has been confirmed by the analysis of debates. It remains to be seen whether a further consideration of the percentages of debates affords any additional support to the other conclusions.

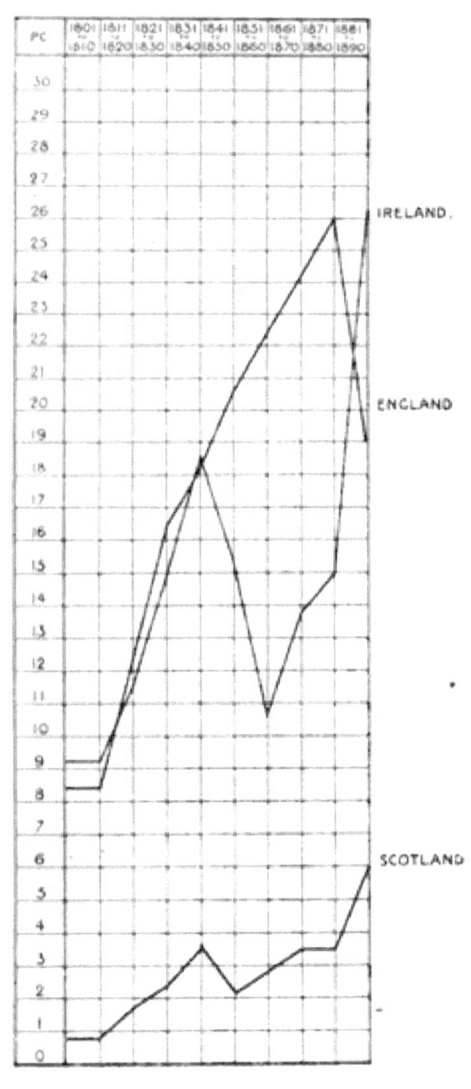

The accompanying diagram represents the course of debates in relation to questions affecting the three States.

Another conclusion, namely, that England is rapidly absorbing the lion's share of the time at the disposal of the House of Commons, is abundantly confirmed by this diagram. It shows clearly the great increase in the percentage of debates in relation to the affairs of England. It is only in the last decade that she sacrifices her pre-eminence to Ireland. But no evidence is afforded that this English increase has been obtained at the expense of the other States. There is no inverse pulsation whatever between the English line and that of Scotland or of Ireland; nor would there be between it and the line representing the total percentage of Scotch and Irish debates; for the characteristic rise and fall of the Irish line is not affected by the inclusion of the Scotch totals.

It is perhaps unreasonable to expect to find any evidence of such a competition. It is far easier to force a debate upon the House of Commons than to carry a bill through it. Neither the Scotch nor the Irish section is strong enough to insist upon legislation in accordance with its wishes, but both have the power of compelling a debate upon matters affecting their interests. In fact, a large number of the debates which have, during the last thirty years, combined to swell the Scotch and Irish totals have originated in the discontent of the Irish members with the legislation which has been forced upon them, and of the Scotch members because they were unable to obtain the legislation which they desired. The smaller States are not at the mercy of England in this respect as they are in regard to legislation.

The class of debate which has suffered from the over-pressure of Parliament must therefore be sought in the Federal section. The accompanying diagrams represent (1) the decrease of the percentage of total federal debates; (2) the decrease of the percentage of debates relating to the United Kingdom, and (3) the decrease of the percentage of debates relating to foreign and colonial affairs.

Diagram I., therefore, represents the totals of the figures depicted in diagrams II. and III. It will be seen that the addition of the foreign and colonial debates to the debates relating to the United Kingdom, although their amount is proportionately small, varies the course of the line to a very considerable extent. In four decades out of eight it actually deflects it. On the other hand, a comparison of the line of foreign and colonial debates in the third diagram

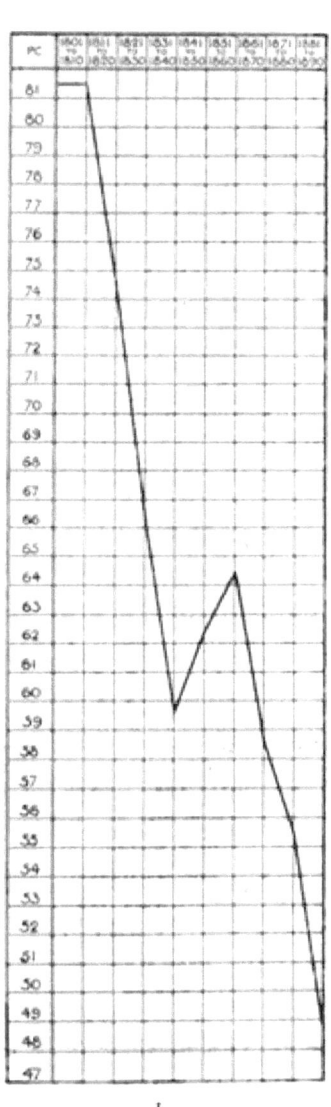

I.

with the line of total federal debates in the first shows a practical correspondence. The character of the line of total federal debates is therefore determined, not by its larger factor, the debates relating to the United Kingdom, but by the comparatively insignificant percentage of the foreign and colonial debates. In other words, it is possible to subtract from the total federal percentage the whole of the share of the United Kingdom without altering its fluctuations to any appreciable extent.

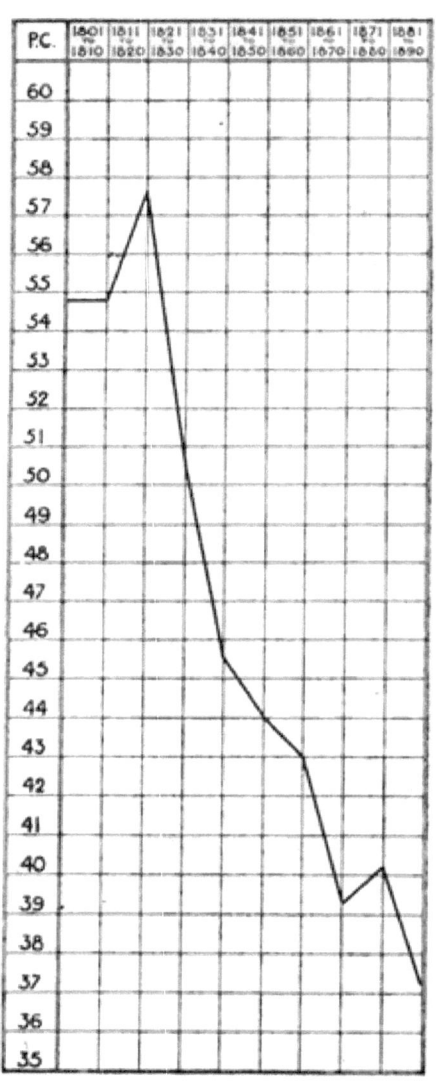

II.

In the third diagram the fluctuations of the percentages of Irish debates are represented by a thin dotted line. It will be remembered that this line represents also in character the line of the total percentages of Scotch and Irish debates. The addition of the Scotch percentage would alter its position, but would not alter its characteristic fluctuations. This diagram shows that there is a very definite inverse pulsation between the percentages of Irish and of foreign and colonial debates; but since the line of foreign and colonial debates is characteristic of the line of total federal debates, it follows that there is a similar inverse pulsation between it and the Irish or the Irish and Scotch line. There is, however, no such inverse pulsation between those lines and the line representing the percentage of debates relating to the United Kingdom

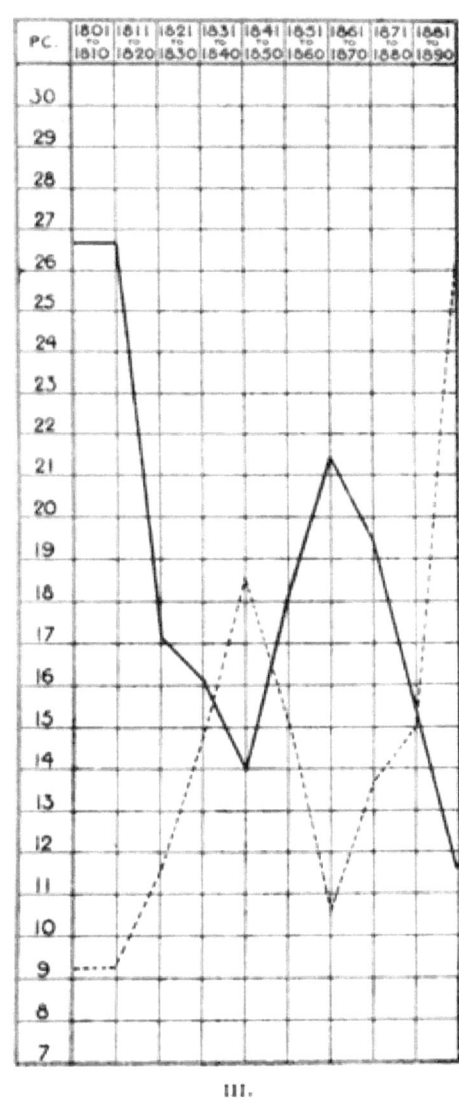

III.

in diagram II. In four decades out of eight these lines correspond. The conclusion to be drawn from these facts is that the absorption by Irish (and possibly Scotch) debates of the time of the House of Commons has been at the expense of the consideration of foreign and colonial affairs. And the evidence of this fact is the more decisive and remarkable because in no decade except the last does the sum of all these classes of debates amount to more than 37·0 per cent., or rather more than one-third of the total.

A little consideration will show the antecedent probability of the fact which the figures have demonstrated. There have always been parties in Parliament strong enough and eager enough to insist upon the full discussion of "States" questions and of questions relating to the United Kingdom, but there never has been any party especially interested in promoting foreign and colonial debates. When pressure was exerted for the purpose of securing discussions upon matters affecting the minor States, and more particularly Ireland, it naturally travelled in the line of least resistance, and absorbed the time which would otherwise have been devoted to the discussion of subjects which were under no organised parliamentary protection.

The figures have therefore disclosed a further and most serious disability which has been imposed upon Parliament by the constitution of

1800; a disability which every man who is not an avowed member of the "Little England" party must view with regret and alarm. The intrusion of Irish debates upon the time of the House of Commons has paralysed that House in those functions which are most conspicuously federal and imperial. The time which should have been devoted to the consideration of questions which vitally affect national interests of the largest magnitude, during a period of immense colonial expansion, which has brought us into closer and more complicated relations with most civilised nations and with numerous barbarous tribes, has been limited by the pressure of the demand for discussions upon questions of comparatively local importance, in regard to which the majority of members have little knowledge and less interest. The upholders of the sacro-sanctity of the constitution of 1800 are wont to contend that the maintenance of that constitution is essential to the greatness, if not of the existence, of the Empire. As a matter of fact, the Union with Ireland has been the prime cause of the recent neglect of great questions of national policy by the House of Commons, a neglect which is increasing until it threatens to become disastrous. If the attention of the House of Commons is in the future to be more and more deflected from these imperial topics, in the right solution of which the welfare of the nation is so deeply involved, and is to be increasingly concentrated upon questions which, relatively, are of merely parochial importance, Parliament will, not long hence, entirely lose control of the vaster national destinies. The fact is a pregnant one for those who believe that those destinies depend upon the maintenance of the policy of 1800. If no other failure could be alleged against that policy, this single defect should convince them of the necessity for relieving the " Federal " Parliament from the burden of the rapidly-increasing business of the component States.

CHAPTER VI

THE DANGER TO THE CONSTITUTION

ALTHOUGH the consideration of so many figures must of necessity have proved wearisome, the conclusions which have been derived from them are not without value in the attempt to estimate the strength of the forces which make for a constitutional change in the direction of Federation. They form a ground-work of fact which will enable us, later on, to test the validity of certain objections to the adoption of a federal constitution for the United Kingdom. In such an investigation as the present, occasional repetition is inevitable, and it will be well, before proceeding to the next branch of our subject, namely, the constitutional dangers which result from the conditions revealed by our analysis of the legislative and deliberative functions of Parliament, to sum up once more the definite information which we have gained.

We have discovered, first, that both in matters of legislation and in matters of debate the separate interests of the States which compose the United Kingdom have been thrusting themselves more and more upon the attention of Parliament, while the joint, or federal, interests have been falling into the background; second, that the growth of States legislation has been largely due to the increasing needs of England; third, that Scotland and Ireland have been compelled to struggle against England and against each other for a limited share of legislation, and that, in consequence, the representatives of those States have been compelled in sheer self-defence "to safeguard the interests" of their "particular localities or countries;" fourth, that during the decade 1851-1860 the amount of business, both legislative and administrative, became so enormous that Parliament was incapable of transacting the whole of it efficiently—that is, Parliament was afflicted with partial paralysis; fifth, that the intrusion of discussions upon Irish affairs into the House of Commons has tended to paralyse that House in its efficient control over our foreign and colonial policy, over that portion of our political activity which is most essentially imperial.[1]

We pass now to consider some of the constitutional dangers which have resulted from these conditions, and none can more fitly head the list, both on account of its magnitude and

---

[1] That is to say, we have confirmed, by a separate line of evidence, propositions 1, 2 and 3. See *ante*, p. 20.

its far-reaching consequences, than that which has been last mentioned. We have already noted how marvellously during the present century, and more especially of recent years, our colonial interests have developed, and how, in consequence, our relations with foreign powers have become closer and more complicated. We not unreasonably expected to find that Parliament would be paying more and more attention to these subjects, but we discover, on the contrary, that pressure from one small island has compelled the House of Commons to neglect or to ignore them. It is precisely since the decade 1851-60 —the decade in which we have ascertained that parliamentary over-pressure commenced—that we find that these foreign and colonial debates have dropped from their highest to their lowest percentage.

It is inconceivable that any man, who has the interests of our great Empire at heart, who is proud of the colonies which our industry and perseverance have founded, who desires to draw these magnificent dependencies into closer union with the mother-country, can view such a result otherwise than with alarm and dismay. And even those who have no faith in the policy of colonial expansion will probably admit that it is a disaster that Parliament should lose control over these questions. They involve considerations of the most vital importance to the nation—questions of peace and war; questions which affect our commercial relations and the prosperity of trade; questions of finance. There is not a nerve in the whole body politic which may not be numbed into inanition if Parliament is paralysed in these functions. If the House of Commons cannot discuss them it cannot understand them, and if it cannot understand them it is not likely that it will deal wisely with them when a sudden emergency arises, calling for prompt decision.

It may be urged that a growing sense of the necessity for continuity in foreign policy has resulted in an increasing reticence upon such questions. This may be the case to some slight extent, but a perusal of the debates upon foreign affairs which have taken place during the last forty years does not lend much support to the assumption. Moreover, the contention does not account for the concurrent decrease in the debates upon colonial subjects, for upon these no such reticence is essential.

It may also be urged that contemporary conditions must affect the percentage of these debates; that they will be higher during periods of war than during periods of peace. There is some truth in the assertion; let us, therefore, endeavour to ascertain how much. In the decade 1851-60 this class of debates reached its highest point. The foreign and colonial debates amounted to 21·4 per cent. of the total. That decade covers the period of the Crimean War and of the Indian Mutiny, so the contemporary conditions tended to swell both sections simultaneously. The percentage of the previous decade was 18·1; that of the subsequent decade 19·5. The Crimean War and the Indian Mutiny therefore increased this class of debate very slightly. Neither of the objections, to which reference has been made, is of sufficient force to invalidate the conclusion which we have drawn from the statistics; namely, that the effect of the constitution of 1800 has been to produce a partial and growing paralysis of Parliament in its dealings with foreign and colonial affairs.

This danger affects the whole of our external relations, but other dangers have arisen in regard to the internal relations of the three kingdoms, which, although they are not so far-reaching in their consequences, are of none the less serious import. The doctrine that lies at the basis of constitutional government is that no law shall be enforceable without the consent of the majority of the representatives of those who will be affected by it. It is a doctrine which England upheld with no uncertain voice during the greater part of the seventeenth century, and to maintain it she encountered the chances and dangers of two revolutions. When the Parliament of 1628 commenced the long conflict against Charles I. by adopting the Petition of Right, it declared that "acts had been done not warrantable by the laws and statutes of this realm." When the Parliament of 1689 sought to justify the revolution which placed William of Orange upon the English throne, it enumerated, in the Bill of Rights, acts which had been done which were infringements of "the laws and liberties of this realm." The intention in both cases was to declare, with as great emphasis as possible, that by no device, whether by proclamation, by ordinance, by the exercise of the dispensing power, or by unauthorised levying of taxes, should any command be enforced without the sanction of Parliament. But at that time the House of Commons represented England only. The consent of that House to any new law meant the consent of the majority of the representatives of those who would be bound to obey that law. This is not a doctrine which has become obsolete or inapplicable because the conditions which rendered it necessary have changed. On the contrary, the endeavour has always been, and still is, to make Parliament as accurate a representation as possible of the political opinions of the electorate. It is a doctrine which must be observed in any well-ordered democracy. No school of constitutional theorists has yet arisen to advocate that a government, ostensibly based upon the will of the majority, should, in fact, give effect to the will of the minority, and it does not seem worth while to labour the argument that such a scheme would be productive of dissatisfaction and of unrest. But, salutary as the doctrine is, it is nevertheless being gradually destroyed, because one of the results of the Acts of Union has been to give members of the House of Commons the right to vote upon bills which do not affect the interests of the nationalities which they represent—to aid in passing laws which their constituents will not be compelled to obey. If such legislation were rare, the fact would not be of much importance, but, as we have seen, it is very frequent. The only laws to which the doctrine now applies are the "Federal" laws, which bind the whole of the United Kingdom. In all cases of "States" legislation—the constantly increasing class—there exists the possibility, which not infrequently converts itself into fact, that the wishes of the minority of the persons who will be affected by any given law will be imposed upon the majority.

This misfortune may overtake any one of the three States. In the case of Ireland it may be said to have been the permanent political condition. The constitutional theory that laws receive the assent of the majority of the representatives of those who have to obey them has become a fiction. As a general rule Ireland has had no more voice in framing her "State" laws than she would have had if parliamentary representation had been denied her, or if those laws were the proclamations of a Stuart king. The tyrant is no longer a monarch, but a Parliament; the methods with which Ireland is asked to be content are identical with those which England resisted by force of arms. Occasionally there is epidemic in Great Britain a desire to do "justice to Ireland;" the very name of the disease being a satire upon the normal apathy which some Englishmen account health. But even when the epidemic is at its height, our attempts to legislate in accordance with the wish of the Irish people receive, at most, a hesitating support from their elected representatives, and generally fail to satisfy those for whose benefit they are made.

The case of Scotland is not so hard, and consequently her complaints are not so loud. Her grievance against the present system is, not so much that laws are forced upon her against her will, as that she cannot obtain the legislation which her needs require. She has to content herself, if she can, with the legislative crumbs which fall from England's table. In the earlier part of the eighteenth century England did indeed force upon the Scots legislation which was hateful to them, but that is no longer the case. The attitude of modern Governments towards Scotland has been, on the whole, a sincere desire, coupled with an inability, to carry out the wishes of the Scotch members.[1] "Only tell us what you want," Government says to them in effect, "and if you are all agreed, and will promise not to waste time in debate, we will do our best, without pledging ourselves definitely, to get your bill through." That is the burden of numberless replies of ministers to inquiries addressed to them by irritated Scotch members. Nevertheless, there are many unsolved questions which affect Scotland only, such as the Established Church question, which English and Irish members may conceivably settle in a manner opposed to the wishes of the Scotch majority. Scotland is liable at any moment to be subjected to a law which, so far as she is concerned, is merely a parliamentary proclamation.

The disadvantage to which England is subjected by reason of the abrogation of the constitutional doctrine which is under discussion has recently formed a staple of the speeches and writings of prominent politicians who are uncompromising supporters of the system which entails it. It is an indisputable fact that legislation which affects England alone has recently been passed by majorities which have been composed

---

[1] This must only be taken as a statement of a general tendency. At times the Scotch have complained that laws have been forced upon them in opposition to their will. See *post*, p. 170.

of a minority of the English representatives, reinforced by Irish and Scotch members. And there are not a few purely English questions outstanding which may be settled by similar methods. In illustration of this point let us take a question which is not yet within the range of practical politics. Let us suppose that, at some time in the twentieth century, a Government which advocates the disestablishment of the Church of England comes into office, and brings in a bill for that purpose. Let us further suppose—and the supposition is by no means improbable—that the majority of English members are opposed to the measure. On this particular question the Government would be supported by a minority only of the representatives of those whose interests would be affected by an Act for disestablishment. But the bill would be passed nevertheless, because the will of the English majority would be overruled by the votes of Scotch and Irish members, who represent constituencies which have no direct interest in the question, and which will not be in any way affected by the law when it comes into operation.

It is doubtful whether a man could be found who would assert that a measure so carried was an act of justice or of wisdom. The majority of Englishmen would have been coerced into obedience to a law which offended their deepest convictions, and against which their consciences revolted. The vital principle of democratic government would have been flagrantly violated, and the English nation would be alarmed and irritated. Its wishes would have been overwhelmed by extraneous forces as effectually as if the law had been imposed by a foreign domination.

And there is no way out of the difficulty under our present constitution. It may perhaps be urged that Scotch and Irish members might have the decency to abstain from voting on English affairs. We need only imagine the result of an appeal by Ireland to England and Scotland to apply the same principle to Irish State legislation, to find one conclusive answer to such a proposal. Besides, if such a plan were adopted, no Government would last six weeks, except in the most improbable of all events; namely, that it commanded a majority in each of the three kingdoms. When Irish and Scotch majorities support a Government which is in a minority in England, they do so because the Irish and Scotch State policy of that Government meets with their approval. If it were suggested to them that they ought in justice to refrain from voting for the disestablishment of the English Church because a majority of English members were opposed to it, they would begin to count the cost. They would see that if they refrained from voting they would be contributing to the defeat of a Government whose Irish and Scotch policy satisfied them, and perhaps aiding the advent to power of a Government which would reverse that policy. They would be more than human if they consented to sacrifice the interests of the State which they represented for the sake of the interests of one which they did not represent, even though all the professors in the universe assured them that it was not their duty "to safeguard the interests of particular countries." They would be certain to be found voting steadily in favour of the Government proposals, and in so doing they would be voting, not upon the merits of the bill before the House, but in order to secure other objects which were not then under consideration.

It is not to be supposed that the House of Lords, or indeed any second chamber, would act as an effective check upon such an evil. The Lords could hardly mitigate it if they adopted the even-handed principle of rejecting all State legislation which had not been supported by a State majority in the House of Commons. The House of Lords would probably reject our imagined bill because it is in fact an English House of Lords, bent on "safeguarding the interests of that particular country;" but the idea of that House rejecting an Irish bill because it had not been supported by a majority of Irish members verges upon the ludicrous. The Irish bills which the House of Lords persistently rejects are precisely those rare measures which find their way to the Upper House with the support of the Irish majority.

But let us assume that the House of Lords rejected the Disestablishment Bill; let us even assume that they persisted in rejecting it, session after session, until a general election took place. What would be the probable result? English candidates would go to the country upon a question which affected the interests of their constituents, and the election would turn on disestablishment. If a majority of English electors were still opposed to that policy, a majority of English members would be returned who were pledged to vote against it. But what would be the issue in Ireland and Scotland? Candidates who had voted for the disestablishment of the English Church would point triumphantly to the results which had been achieved in the last Parliament. "We have kept a Government in power," they would boast, "which has carried out your wishes. By doing so we have secured such and such beneficial legislation, this and that administrative reform. If we had voted against the disestablishment of the English Church, and the bill had been lost, the Government would have resigned, and with them might have disappeared all chance of securing those useful reforms which you now enjoy. If you return us again we shall pursue the same policy. We shall 'safeguard the interests of your particular country,' and in order to do so we shall vote for the disestablishment of the English Church." It is unreasonable to suppose that such candidates would lose support for such a policy. In all probability they would return to Westminster with undiminished numbers; and although England—the only country interested in the measure—had returned an emphatic " no " to the appeal made to her, unless her " no " had been so emphatic that her majority swamped the Scotch and Irish majorities, the House of Commons would send the bill up once more to the House of Lords. On no constitutional theory that has ever been broached could the second chamber again reject it. They would have to accept it, and the majority in England would be subjected to the will of the minority.

Perhaps some half-convinced reader may exclaim that the argument is only a re-statement of the weakness which is very generally alleged against popular governments, namely, that representatives will support one item of policy of which they do not approve in order to secure the continuity of a general course of policy of which they do approve—a defect which is inherent in representative institutions.

Let us see if the objection has any solid

foundation. We will test it by another hypothetical case. We will suppose that Government introduces a bill to compel every male person in the United Kingdom to serve for three years in the army. This is what we have called a "federal" bill. We will suppose also that the reader is a member of Parliament, sitting on the Government side of the House, whether for a constituency in England, Scotland or Ireland, it matters not. You are not in favour of the principle of the bill, but you are reluctant to give a vote which might help to overthrow the ministry. The first question that you ask yourself is, "What will my constituents say?" You telegraph to one or two of your supporters to ask them to inquire into the local feeling. A day or two after the first reading you begin to receive letters of remonstrance from electors. In the local newspaper you read a flaming article about the impending subversion of our liberties by the introduction of foreign tyranny in its most hideous and repulsive form. Then you hear from your friends in the constituency that your opponent is going to call an indignation meeting to denounce the measure, and that it is likely to be well attended; in fact, that if you vote for conscription your prospects of success at the next election are gloomy. At this point you seek an interview with the Government Whip. You dilate upon your enthusiasm for the Administration, upon the sacrifices which you have made, and are prepared to make, in support of it. Then, having exhausted your stock of pleasant expressions of esteem and regard, you gently hint that you will certainly be compelled to abstain from voting upon the second reading of the Conscription Bill, even if you do not feel bound to vote against it.

It is evident that if the whole of the nation will be affected by proposed legislation, it can only be in regard to very minor questions that members are able to sacrifice their convictions for the sake of retaining in power a Government whose general policy they approve. They are able to do so merely because the question is so trivial that they can trust their constituents either to ignore or to condone their action. But a federal proposal of the first importance sends a thrill from the centre to all the extremities of the body politic. Every nerve vibrates with excitement, and the political brain is so sensitive that it receives and records the result of the shock instinctively. It is well-nigh impossible for the House of Commons to pass a federal bill to which the majority of the nation is opposed. But the case of States legislation is quite different. When a first-class proposal relating to any one of them is brought forward, two sets of nerve centres are liable to become paralysed. In the supposed case of the Church Disestablishment Bill, Irish and Scotch members would support the Government, not because the question was so unimportant that they could trust their constituents not to call them to account for their action, but because, notwithstanding the fact that it was of overwhelming importance, their constituents had no interest whatever in the question, except that their representatives should so deal with it that questions in which they were interested might be furthered. The forces which usually keep Parliament in touch with the wishes of the nation are inoperative.

It may be objected that although a bill may directly affect only the inhabitants of one of the three States, the principle underlying the bill may be applicable to the others, and that therefore, in voting for the bill, the representatives of the unaffected States are in fact voting for its extension, by a series of States bills, to the whole of the nation, and the question is, on that account, in reality "federal." This objection applies more particularly to the States questions of England and Scotland, because their interests are more identical than those of either of them with Ireland. But it does not remove the difficulty. Suppose that Scotland were in favour of Church Disestablishment, and England were opposed to it. Scotch members would vote for the disestablishment of the English Church in order to create a precedent for the disestablishment of the Church of Scotland, and would in so doing assist in overriding the wishes of England.

Thus we see that our present system of government, which is ostensibly based upon the theory that the will of the majority ought to prevail, is, in fact, so far as the affairs of each State are concerned, an ingenious device for enabling the minority to triumph. England, Ireland and Scotland are, each in their turn, liable to be subjected to legislation which they would reject if the opinion of those who have to obey the law were alone consulted. They are subjected to it by irresponsible persons, who themselves stand outside the scope of it. Legislation carried in such a fashion is as much an act of tyranny as if it were imposed by a royal proclamation or a republican ordinance. If the will of the majority is overridden, it does not much matter whether that result is achieved by one tyrant or by many. The facts remain the same; the very basis of our constitution is sapped.

There are collateral evils attendant upon our present system, which have been more than hinted at in the description of its main defect, and may therefore be discussed with brevity. The reader cannot fail to have noticed how greatly the direct responsibility of members of the House of Commons for their votes has been undermined. In the old English Parliament each member was directly responsible to his constituents for all his parliamentary acts, because all those acts directly affected their interests. Even in such small matters as local legislation this responsibility was accentuated by the custom of referring local bills to committees composed of members for the area affected by them. On no question could any man vote, except the rare cases of Irish legislation, without being liable to be called to account by constituents who had an actual or potential interest in the right solution of that question. But now, upon an increasingly large number of questions, members are free to vote as they see fit, knowing that they will never have to render an account of their stewardship before any such tribunal. English and Scotch constituencies do not trouble themselves about an Irish Municipal Corporation Reform Bill. English and Irish constituencies know little or nothing concerning the Scotch Crofters' Bill. Scotch and Irish constituencies never hear, or want to hear, of a bill for improving English elementary education. And why should they? These matters, interesting enough to the States concerned, in no way affect the interests of the others. On all such topics the members of the States excluded from the bill are free to vote as they like, knowing that a day of reckoning for that vote will never come. They are politically irresponsible, and they frequently use their irresponsible power, as we have seen, for the purpose of furthering interests which are directly entrusted to them, and not for the purpose of settling the measure before them in accordance with reason, justice, and the wishes of those who will have to obey its provisions.

The results of this lack of responsibility are curious. A new word has lately been imported into our vocabulary which has been derived from a meritorious practice of mutual assistance in vogue among American tree-fellers. It was first used in connection with literature, but it has recently been added to our political nomenclature, and in both cases it has suffered degradation in the transfer. "Log-rolling" in politics signifies a practice which is the reverse of meritorious. It is accomplished after this fashion. A group of members for one State, representing possibly the opinion of the minority in that State, support a certain State bill. They know that they are powerless of themselves to pass it; powerless even, owing to the congestion of parliamentary business, to bring it to the dignity of a second reading. They therefore approach members for the other States, and they say, in effect, "Here is a little bill that we want to pass. It does not affect your constituents in the least degree. Will you support it?" And the reply is, "Gentlemen, you are manifestly the best judges of the kind of legislation which is desired by your constituents. We haven't time to master the details of your proposal: we accept your account of its merits; but—the fact is that we are also interested in a little bill which will not touch your constituents. If you could see your way to support us, we, on the other hand, could conscientiously vote for the measure which you have so much at heart." The apparent volume of parliamentary opinion in favour of any given measure is often largely fictitious because such tactics have been adopted, and it becomes an entirely misleading index of the real strength of the forces in favour of that measure.

There is another evil which is the very opposite of log-rolling. It is one which from its nature afflicts the Forward party in the State more keenly than the other, but it is nevertheless a national disadvantage. When the nation has placed that particular party in power, it is an evil if the various schemes for reform which it advocates cannot be put through the winnowing-machine of parliamentary discussion and investigation with the least possible delay. But owing to the congestion of Parliament, questions of this sort are sometimes postponed for years. Now every such question is supported by a band of earnest persons who are called enthusiasts or fanatics, according to the point of view from which their exertions are regarded. By whatever name we may label them, they are generally persons whose political perspective is somewhat distorted. Their own peculiar measure always occupies the political foreground; all others are blended in the hazy distance to form an agreeable contrast to it. They resent an attempt to bring any of the latter into greater prominence as superfluous and impertinent. In such circumstances some sections of these enthusiasts are necessarily doomed to disappointment, and as session after session passes, and their favourite measure still remains blocked with the mass of other bills with which Parliament is incompetent, for want of time, to deal, they grow restive. They begin by muttering threats, and if these prove unavailing, they betake themselves to caves. They revenge their want of success by voting against the Government, regardless of the merits of the question upon which they vote.

This action, which tends to form groups rather than parties in Parliament, is generally adopted by the advocates of "State" bills, because that class of bills is the more numerous, and touches more closely the social wants of the people affected by them. To those who regard politics merely as a game played between political parties, the formation of groups claiming more or less political independence may add greater zest to the diversion. A more far-sighted view will reveal in the tendency a possible germ of decay in our system of constitutional government. The lieutenant who will head a desertion to the enemy because he is not allowed to act as commander-in-chief is likely to betray his new allegiance for the same reason. With the accumulation of undecided questions such semi-independent bands are likely to become more numerous, until continuity of administration is rendered impossible.

We have found, therefore, that three great internal constitutional evils result from our present system of government. First, the destruction in many cases of the doctrine that the governed should assent through their representatives to the laws which they are compelled to obey; second, the sapping of the responsibility of members of the House of Commons for their votes; and third, the provocation to form political groups rather than political parties. The first is, from the point of view of pure constitutionalism, of the greatest importance, and, before passing to another branch of the subject, I must briefly allude to an objection that may at first sight appear to go to the root of the whole argument upon which it is based. It has been urged by writers of distinction that the doctrine of government by the consent of the governed is a snare, a delusion and a farce; that it is gradually eating away the foundations of order and authority; and that it will ultimately lead those who are beguiled by it to the morass of anarchy, from which the only escape will be by aid of the strong hand of despotism. If this contention has any force in it, it would go far to justify a system of government which tended to give effect to the will of minorities.

Foremost among the advocates of this doctrine was the late Mr. J. A. Froude, and his exposition is the more interesting because he admitted, on the other hand, that despotisms invariably lapse into depravity and corruptness, and are necessarily subverted by the people whom they oppress. He saw no progress in political history, only an eternal swing of the pendulum between the curse of despotic injustice and the curse of democratic incompetence. He was the Schopenhauer of politics.

Let us consider Mr. Froude's statement of his case. "Who is free? asks the modern liberal politician, and he answers, The man who has a voice in making the laws which he is expected to obey. . . . That nation is the most free where the laws, by whomsoever framed, correspond most nearly to the will of the Maker of the Universe, by whom, and not by human suffrage, the code of rules is laid down for our obedience. That nation is most a slave which has ceased to believe that such divinely-appointed laws exist, and which will only be bound by the Acts which it places upon its Statute-book."[1]

[1] "English in Ireland," Book VII., c. 1, sect. 2.

The curious confusion contained in the latter part of the quotation is worth noting. It is implied, either that all law should include all morality, or that a nation which is self-governed will obey no moral law which has not received a legal sanction. Mr. Froude's command of exquisite language is too frequently debased to the purpose of casting a fictitious glamour over propositions which need only to be stated in homely terms to stand revealed in naked absurdity.

But let us try, with reverence, to get to the kernel of the contention. It is that the nation is free which obeys laws that are consonant with the will of the Almighty; and there is the concurrent implication that laws which are consonant with the will of the majority of the persons who are expected to obey them are likely to clash with that will, and therefore people who are so governed will not be free.

It is always well to test such theorising by the touchstone of fact. Without going further afield than our own country, let us consider the conflict between English and Scotch law in matters very closely related to the domain of morals. In Scotland relations between man and woman, which, according to English law, would be treated as illicit and unhallowed, are endowed with all the sanctity of marriage. In Scotland illegitimate children of parents who subsequently marry are treated as if they had been born in wedlock; in England they remain bastards. These conflicting laws cannot all correspond with the "will of the Maker of the Universe." Which then is the free nation and which the slave, England or Scotland?

The argument is not tenable even in regard to laws which relate to the domain of morals; but, as a matter of fact, law deals to a far greater extent with questions of expediency than with morals. We cannot conceive of an appeal to the will of the Maker of the Universe upon such questions as the mode of raising revenue, whether it should be by income-tax or excise; whether an agreement should be valid which was not made in writing; the propriety of administering poor relief by means of old age pensions; or what forms of investment should be available for trustees. By far the greater part of our legislation crawls along the dull level road of political expediency. And one vital element in the question of expediency is whether the people who are expected to obey the law are ready to acquiesce in it. Let us test our position by a case. No one now disputes that some system of national education is desirable. It might even be contended that it is consonant with the will of the Maker of the Universe that His creatures should be free to develop the faculties with which He has endowed them, and that therefore a nation, if it is to be free, ought to be compelled at all hazards to educate itself. But suppose such a law were imposed upon a people who were not convinced of its advantages. Their freedom would manifest itself in discontent, in hostility to the benevolence which had forced the law upon them, and in ingenious devices to avoid its provisions; in a very clear demonstration, in fact, that they considered themselves little better than slaves. No law, however excellent in its ideal, will prove beneficial, or perhaps even enforceable, unless it accords with the wishes of a majority of those who have to obey it. The assent, if not the consent, of those who are governed must in the long run regulate legislation in a civilised State, although measures which the people resent may for a time be enforced. The virtue of frank recognition of the consent of the people as the basis of all government is that it acts as a compensating balance. It prevents the legislature from paralysing the nation by falling too far behind its average opinion, and from rendering its own action futile by rushing too far ahead of that opinion. It is the only sure foundation upon which to build a peaceful and orderly polity.

I have dwelt upon this perverse theory because persons who are fascinated by a copious vocabulary and by well-balanced periods are apt to be seduced into believing that they necessarily embody a truth which almost amounts to a revelation. Mr. Froude's reasoning would persuade such persons that the practice of government by consent of the governed is responsible for those very evils which we have shown to have been caused by a neglect of it. But the fact that the laws of the United Kingdom, so far as they relate to the three component States, are sometimes enacted in opposition to the will of the majority of those who will have to obey them, can bring small comfort to the believers in a Froudesque constitution. Mr. Froude's contention is that the majority in any given State is unfit, as a rule, to control the affairs of that State. In another characteristic passage, too long for quotation, but which is worth careful perusal, Mr. Froude has more fully elaborated his wonderful theory. In it he remarks: "Only at critical moments, when some patent wrong has to be redressed, will the better kind of men leave their proper occupations to meddle with politics. The peasant and the artisan, the man of business and the man of science, all of all sorts who are good in their kind, give themselves to their own work, caring only to do well what nature has assigned them to do. The volunteer politicians of every class, *those who put themselves forward in elections to choose or to be chosen*, are usually the vain, the restless, the personally ambitious."[1] It is marvellous to what depths the very superior person may descend if he will only give his great intellect entirely to the task. The seventy-five per cent. of the electorate who,

[1] "The English in Ireland," Book VIII., c. 1, sect. 1.

as a rule, take part in electing the House of Commons are restless, vain, ambitious persons. The residue, who, except upon extraordinary occasions, remain absorbed in personal interests and avocations, who take no thought for the common good or for the welfare of their fellow citizens, who solve all such problems by the old query, "Am I my brother's keeper?"—these, apparently, are the salt of the earth, and should bear political rule.

But although such grotesque reasoning might point to the presumption that, let us say, our imagined bill for the disestablishment of the English Church corresponded with "the will of the Maker of the Universe," for the simple reason that a majority of the vain, restless and ambitious persons who would be affected by it were opposed to its provisions, and were therefore almost certain to be wrong, the argument would at once be smitten sterile by the fact that other majorities of equally vain, restless and ambitious persons from other countries were in favour of that policy. Unless we are to lapse into mere incoherence, we are bound to presume that they are also wrong, and that the views of the minorities in those countries are in accordance with the will of the Almighty. Thus we find ourselves landed in a dilemma, from which there is no way of escape.

But the point for anyone who may still cling

to the Froude doctrine of government is this: If the people, recording their opinions by means of the suffrage, are incompetent to manage affairs which affect their interests and which they understand, how can they be competent to manage the affairs of other people? The vain, restless, ambitious English cannot suddenly become heaven-sent rulers the moment they divert their attention from their own concerns to those of Scotland and Ireland; nor will any special illumination be vouchsafed to the Scotch and Irish when they meddle with English business. No miracle will transform them from such ignoble creatures as Mr. Froude has depicted them into the enlightened dictators for which the soul of the Froudist yearns. He can find no consolation whatever in the fact that our present constitution facilitates the imposition of the will of the minority upon the majority.

The true patriot and leader of men is he who neither wastes his own energy in a struggle after impossible ideals which are beautiful in proportion to their vagueness, nor curbs the energies of others by an endeavour to shackle them to the burdensome precedents of the past; but who recognises within the polity of his country the germ of life and growth, and who strives to cherish the living good by relieving it of that encumbrance of dead tradition which inevitably accompanies healthy development.

III

THE BURDENS OF THE STATES

8

CHAPTER VII

THE BURDEN OF ENGLAND

HITHERTO we have been investigating our subject from what may be termed the internal standpoint. We have taken our stand upon the floor of the House of Commons; we have noted the working of its mechanism and we have digested and tabulated the results of our observations. But it may fairly be said, "This is all very ingenious, and perhaps interesting to people who find mental relaxation in the study of averages and percentages, but it is pure theory. It is easy to prove the existence of intolerable evils upon paper, but the force of the evidence is considerably lessened if it be found that they are tolerated with equanimity by the people whom they are supposed to afflict. You have said that the constitutional defects which you profess to have discovered must be productive of dissatisfaction and unrest. To complete your argument you must prove that those evils have actually been generated. As to Ireland, we know that she is dissatisfied and restless. She was the same when she controlled her own affairs; she always has been, and probably always will be. But where is the evidence of dissatisfaction in England and Scotland? If they are content, may we not apply your own argument about majorities to nations as well as to individuals, and conclude that the assent of two countries should overrule the opposition of the third?"

That Ireland has always been restless and dissatisfied, and probably, under existing conditions, will always remain so, may readily be admitted. The case of Ireland involves so many complicated considerations, and is so difficult to touch upon without provoking political strife, that it will be safer to postpone it until we have ascertained how far it is true that England and Scotland are thoroughly satisfied with the working of our present constitution.

Is England satisfied? It would perhaps be more accurate to describe her attitude as one of doubt, rather than of confirmed dissatisfaction. Her position as predominant partner gives her political advantages which are denied to the juniors. Out of a total of 670 members she returns 495. The remaining 175 members are returned by Scotland and Ireland. England can, if she is so minded, overwhelm by numerical force the contingents of the other two States, even if every Scotch and Irish member were returned pledged to vote with the English minority. There exists the possibility, therefore, for England to assert the will of her majority, which does not exist for Ireland and Scotland. Those two countries can only assert the will of their respective majorities in the event of the return of an English majority of their way of thinking, or an English minority sufficiently large to make up a majority in alliance with the Scotch and Irish. But it is in precisely the latter event that England is liable to be governed according to the will of her minority, and it is on such occasions that she becomes conscious of the evil which more permanently afflicts the other two countries.

It cannot be doubted that the chance that England may be exposed to this disadvantage has been largely increased since 1885. The Franchise and Redistribution Acts of that year made the Irish representation for the first time a fairly accurate reflection of Irish political opinion. They paved the way for the return of an overwhelming majority of Irish members, who, although they have not pledged themselves to support any English party, have since that date usually acted with the English minority. There is no probability that this Irish majority will be materially reduced by any change of Irish opinion, and the consequence is that when the English majority is opposed by the Irish majority it has a greater leeway to make up in order to assert the will of England.

It may be said indeed that it is only during the existence of the Parliament of 1892-95 that England has been subjected, in English State matters, to the will of the minority of her electors. No one will dispute that, if the English members alone had decided the fate of the English State legislation which was passed by that Parliament, much of it would never have become law, or would have become law in a very different form. And it is precisely during that period that English discontent has become articulate. Dissatisfaction with a faulty constitution is a force which develops slowly. It takes time for men to realise the failure. As an eminent Scotch statesman once declared, " These things begin in a whisper, but the whisper grows into a loud voice, which those who are wise will stop to listen to before it develops into a sullen roar."[1] I am inclined to think that in England public opinion has nearly reached the second stage indicated in this passage. She has passed the period of whispering her discontent and she is beginning to speak with a loud voice—a somewhat incoherent voice, it is true, because she fails to comprehend, at present, the real cause of her displeasure; but a voice not without sound and fury in it, nevertheless. It was hardly possible during a session of the late Parliament to take up any newspaper which supports the

[1] The Marquess of Lothian. Hansard, vol. 299, c. 95.

retention of our present constitutional system without finding contemptuous or irritable allusions to the fact that, in certain divisions, the will of the English majority had been over-ridden. English members of eminence who oppose constitutional change are never tired of dinning the same complaint into the ears of their constituents, as if it were the fault of the Irish and Scotch representatives, and not of the system under which we are governed. It has been crystallised into epigram by a very high political authority. The English are suffering, we are told, from the domination of a " Celtic fringe."[1] Her reasonable Anglo-Saxon desires in regard to legislation are defeated by the irruption into Parliament of these outsiders. What can such complaints mean but that reason and justice demand that England should decide questions which affect her solely without extraneous interference? If that be the basis of the contention, it is difficult to see how any man, whatever may be his political convictions, can fail to sympathise with it. The only fault to be found with the proposition is that it is incomplete. It fails to recognise that the same sense of injustice under which England sometimes smarts afflicts Scotland and Ireland on other occasions. There are times when these two countries make precisely the same complaint, alleging that they cannot obtain the legislation

---

[1] See Lord Salisbury's speech at Belfast, May 24th, 1893.

which they desire and need because of the oppressive hand of the English majority. The curious thing is that those who so sadly bewail England's cruel fate have never seen anything but absurdity in a similar outcry from the sister kingdoms. To such lamentations they have replied with the assurance that the interests of the three kingdoms are so closely bound up together that they can by no means be separated; all must consult for the good of all. When England finds herself in the same plight, she gets restive, and talks fretfully about Celtic fringes. It would almost seem as if such politicians were striving to carry into practice the old north-country proverb, which describes a self-seeking person as working always with the rake and never with the shovel. They desire some form of constitution, as yet undevised, whereby England shall control her own State affairs without interference from outside, and yet retain her grasp upon the State affairs of her neighbours. There is clearly only one just and logical solution of the difficulty. If England really desires to possess untrammelled control over her State legislation she must perforce concede the same liberty to her partners. If, on the other hand, she is convinced that the disadvantages of local self-government outweigh the disadvantages of an incorporating union, then she must submit to the inconvenience entailed by the latter without vain outcry against it. It is an inconvenience of which she is the author, and which affects the sister kingdoms far more seriously.

Mark the absurd dilemma upon the horns of which the advocates of the present constitution impale themselves. When Irish and Scotch members exercise their undoubted constitutional right to vote upon English State questions, they are confronted by the majestic form of the Prime Minister, who assures them that they are merely Celtic fringes, and exhorts them to content themselves with endeavouring to unravel their own tangles, and not to attempt to meddle with affairs that do not concern them. If the good folk take heed to this precept, and endeavour to obey it, a learned Oxford professor starts up and points out to them that they are acting in a shockingly unconstitutional manner, because it is not their duty "to safeguard the interests of particular countries." Between the politician and the professor, what are the poor fellows to do? They must not interfere with English affairs because they are Celtic fringes; they must not confine themselves to their national interests because that is grossly unconstitutional. The result of the two doctrines appears to be what I have already indicated, namely, that Scotch and Irish members should content themselves with voting supplies, and taking part in that important but somewhat uninteresting section of business which has been termed Federal, and that they should surrender the control of their own State affairs to the management of England. "What union could we have with Great Britain but a union of debt and taxation?"[1] exclaimed an Irish member towards the end of the last century. It would seem as if such a union were the ideal of some modern statesmen.

England has become so far conscious of the disadvantage under which she is labouring that some of her politicians are looking about for a remedy. And they seem to think that they have discovered it in the fact that, proportionately to population, Ireland is over-represented. If the three kingdoms were represented upon a common basis, Ireland would lose about twenty members, and England would gain that number. It is not uninstructive to note that the upholders of the sacro-sanctity of the Act of Union are prepared to violate one of its most vital conditions to serve their own purposes, but the point is of too little importance to claim more than a passing notice. It is more necessary to observe that, although such a measure would doubtless strengthen England's predominance, it would increase, not diminish, the constitutional evil. England would be more capable of overruling the wishes of Ireland and Scotland, and less liable to have her own wishes overruled. But,

[1] Froude's "English in Ireland," Book VII., c. 1, sect. 10.

on the other hand, Scotland and Ireland would be rendered more helpless, and consequently more discontented. It is a proposal for the purpose of asserting the predominance of England, rather than for preserving an equality between the three kingdoms.

Such a proposal could only be made with justice if the whole of the interests of the three kingdoms, or at any rate the vast majority of them, were identical. The advocates of the measure profess to believe that those interests are practically identical. We have already sufficiently exposed the hollowness of that allegation. It may with much more reason be contended that where small States, having separate interests, are forced into an incorporating union with a more populous State, they should, in bare justice, be conceded more than their proportionate share of representatives. We have seen that Scotland and Ireland have a hard struggle to get their needed legislation; if Irish membership were reduced, her struggle would be still more severe. The principle which I have endeavoured to state is one which has been recognised as just by the legislature and by men of business in matters which affect the commercial interests of the community. Almost all the articles of association of limited liability companies[1] provide against the swamping of the wishes of small shareholders

[1] And see also Table A in the Companies' Act, 1862.

by large ones. This is effected by reducing the voting power of a shareholder in regard to any shares which he may hold beyond a certain fixed number. In other words, the voting value of small shareholders is raised as against the "predominant partner," and the justice of the principle has never been impugned.

Although the analogy may not be perfect at all points, the same principle manifestly applies to a partnership of nations. The small partners have an undoubted right to be protected against the overwhelming vote of the large one. This protection is afforded in the most practical manner by the system of making the constituencies of England contain a larger number of electors than those of Scotland and Ireland. It diminishes the voting power of the predominant partner. The facts which have been already adduced prove that a reduction of the voting power of the United Kingdom to one common value would, under our present constitution, be an act of tyranny perpetrated under the name of justice.

England has reason to complain when she is subjected to laws which do not commend themselves to the intelligence of the majority of her electors, but she will go the wrong way to work if she seeks to assert her independent control over her State legislation by reducing the other two kingdoms more nearly to the status of dependent States. That would be the net result of any attempt to place England in such a predominance of voting power that she would assert a more absolute control over, not only her own State legislation, but also the State legislation of the other two countries. Those countries would not then, even in appearance, hold the position of equal partners. They would be reduced to the condition of petitioners for justice, which they had no power to enforce. The only remedy which will not prove a mere concealment of the disease will be found in facing the facts frankly. England desires freedom in the management of those affairs which affect her interests alone; let her take it, and, while taking it, let her concede the same right to those sister countries which have greater need to claim it, and which, having received the boon, will leave federal interests, without reluctance, to federal control.

CHAPTER VIII

THE BURDEN OF SCOTLAND

WE have hitherto been considering the complaints which have arisen in the dominant state of our political union. Those complaints are of recent origin, and are, as yet, scarcely formulated intelligibly. But we have found evidence enough to show that germs of dissatisfaction already exist which may develop into a more definite sentiment of discontent. We now pass from the case of England to that of Scotland, and, therefore, to the consideration of the attitude of one of the minor States towards the incorporating union.

The case of Scotland is one of peculiar interest. It is not, like that of Ireland, a study in morbid political anatomy. In Great Britain the policy of corporate union has had the fairest trial in most advantageous circumstances. Since 1707 Scotland has risen from a social and material condition far lower than the present state of Ireland to a prosperity which rivals that of England. For a long period Scottish opinion was pertinaciously opposed to the Union, but the spirit of revolt was at last succeeded by a spirit of acquiescence. This latter stage was reached before the union with Ireland; that is, before the constitutional change was effected which was the original cause of many of the evils which I have endeavoured to expose. But Scotch acquiescence lasted for a considerable period after the union with Ireland. If the opinion of Scotland has gradually undergone a change, that change cannot be attributed to passion or to inveterate prejudice. Hence the case of Scotland is, as one of her representatives once said, "a peculiarly favourable one to take up . . . . because it is uncomplicated at present with any popular excitement or political feeling."[1] It must be remembered also that the Scotch are by no means an impulsive race. They are much more prone to bear the ills they have than fly to others that they know not of. Moreover, they enjoy a higher average of education, and, perhaps, even of intelligence, than the rest of the United Kingdom, and they are endowed with a keen political instinct. The probability is great, therefore, that any modification of political opinion is due, in such circumstances, to the operation of normal political forces and to the exercise of a sane political judgment.

The political history of Scotland, in relation to the Union, is divisible into three distinct and nearly equal periods: (1) The period of resist-

[1] Sir D. Wedderburn. Hansard, vol. 209, c. 1854.

ance; (2) the period of acquiescence; and (3) the period of dissatisfaction. It will tend to throw light upon the whole question under discussion if we give some consideration to each of these three periods.

The prevalent opinion is that England and Scotland rushed into the embrace of the incorporating union like ardent bridegroom and willing bride. Even so acute an observer as Professor Dicey has given countenance to this view of the case. He has said: "The experience of England and Scotland in the eighteenth century . . . . shows that common national feeling or the sense of common interests may be too strong to allow of that combination of union and separation which is the foundation of federalism."[1]

This opinion is so divergent from the facts of the case, that it is worth while considering whether "a common national feeling," or a "sense of common interests"—the sentiments which should, according to Professor Dicey, form the foundation of an incorporating union—had any existence whatever in the two nations at the time when the Union was effected.

If there was any "common national feeling" between the two countries, it displayed itself in a very eccentric manner, both immediately before 1707 and for many years after. When the Cameronians were not disinclined to make

[1] "The Law of the Constitution," p. 132.

common cause with their hated hereditary foes, the Jacobites, to prevent or to destroy the Union, the instinct of the common nationality of the two countries must have been in a somewhat rudimentary stage of development in Scotland. It could hardly have been an unconquerable feeling of brotherhood towards the Scotch which induced England to make preparations for war against them after the passing of the Act of Security by the Scotch Parliament.[1] Such facts are evidence of the existence of mutual hatred rather than of a common national feeling.

Was the Union then due to " a sense of common interests " ? The reason which induced England to agree to the Union was a sense of danger to herself from the existence of an independent Scotland. That which induced Scotland to consent to it was the conviction of a Scotch national need. In the view of English politicians it was of the last importance to secure the succession of the Protestant house of Hanover to the crowns of both kingdoms in the event of Queen Anne dying childless. It was competent for the Scotch Parliament to regulate the Scotch succession otherwise, and, as a matter of fact, when the irritation between the two countries was at its height, the Scotch Parliament did enact that the successor to the Scotch Crown should not in certain circumstances be the

[1] Burton: "History of Scotland," vol. 8, p. 103.

successor to the English Crown.[1] A hostile independent Scotland, in strict alliance, almost to a certainty, with France, who supported the claim of the Stuarts to the English throne, would be a perpetual menace to English security. England was willing to pay a large price to escape the danger, but Scotland detested the idea of surrendering her independence. The interest which induced England to seek the Union was not, therefore, one which was common to Scotland.

The national need which urged Scotland to accept the Union was the necessity for free trade. Her goods paid customs on entry into England just as if they were the goods of aliens. She was excluded from trade with English colonies. A few years before she had made a frantic attempt at colonisation upon her own account. The Darien expedition had failed, and disastrous loss had overwhelmed the adventurers, because England would not, and Scotland could not, protect them against Spain by force of arms. Scotland became convinced that her only chance of commercial expansion lay in breaking down the English trade monopoly; but this was a concession which England grudged to grant. The political economy of the time assured her that to concede free trade to any other nation was to sacrifice her com-

[1] The Act of Security. Act III. of Session of 1704.

mercial prosperity. The interest which induced Scotland to tolerate the Union was not, therefore, one which was common to England.

Each nation was eager to secure an end which was necessary for its own well-being, but which was hateful to the other, and each unwillingly agreed to surrender the privilege which it valued to purchase the relief which was essential to it. Each, in fact, had a choice of evils presented to it, and accepted the smaller evil of the two. It was a bargain between unfriendly parties, who disliked and feared one another. The " sense of common interests " was conspicuous by its absence. The attitude of both countries towards the Union is well illustrated by a debate which took place in the House of Lords in 1713. The Scotch representative peers brought forward a bill for the dissolution of the Union, for restoring to each kingdom its rights and privileges, and securing the succession of the house of Hanover to the throne of both kingdoms. The Scotch had evidently begun to rue the loss of their Parliament, and to be willing to forego the trade benefits which they had received in exchange for it. At least thirteen out of the sixteen Scotch peers voted for leave to bring in the bill, and on a division it was found that fifty-four peers had voted on each side. The motion was lost on the proxies, of which there were thirteen for and seventeen against it. It appears, therefore, that more than a third of the total number of English peers capable of voting were at that time in favour of a repeal of the Union.[1]

It will be seen that the relations between England and Scotland were such as would naturally have indicated a federal, rather than an incorporating union. England desired unity in succession to the throne, and the consequent unity of foreign policy and of national defence; Scotland sought a customs union, which would enable her trade to expand. The wishes of both countries might have been fulfilled by a federal union, which left both Parliaments in existence to control purely State affairs. How was it then that this political tendency failed to produce its natural result?

We must observe, in the first place, that the popular conception of federal government, namely, a united assembly having control over federal affairs, and local assemblies having control over the affairs of each State, is of comparatively modern origin. The negotiators of the Union had no constitution of the United States of North America to refer to for guidance or for warning during their deliberations. If they sought for precedents they would have had

[1] Parl. Hist., vol. 6, c. 1216. Lords' Journals, vol. 19, p. 556. The House of Lords at that date consisted of about 157 Temporal Lords capable of voting, 26 Bishops, and 16 Scotch representative peers. Parl. Hist., vol. 7, c. 27.

to turn to Holland or to Switzerland. But the peculiar admixture of city and State government in Holland rendered its constitution manifestly inapplicable to the case of England and Scotland; and the politician who chanced to cast an eye towards Switzerland would have concluded that the days of her existence as an independent State were numbered. It would have seemed almost certain that she was falling to pieces: that France would absorb one portion of her territory, Austria perhaps another; and that some of the cantons would form petty semi-independent States under local princelets.[1] It was in 1707 that Neuchâtel accepted the King of Prussia for Duke, to escape the domination of France.

It is true that there was at the time a great talk about an arrangement which was termed a "Fœderal Union," and that Scotland expected that some such arrangement would be effected.[2] But the speeches delivered in the Scots Parliament during the debates upon the Articles of Union show conclusively that the term was used in its original, not in its derivative, sense. Mr. Seton, of Pitmadden, was one of the representatives for the shire of Aberdeen, and also a commissioner for negotiating the Union. He attempted to describe exhaustively the methods by which the

[1] Switzerland was at that time a League rather than a Federation.
[2] Burton's "History of Scotland," vol. 8, p. 119.

questions between the two countries could be settled. These were: (1) "That we continue under the same sovereign as England, with limitations on his prerogative as King of Scotland; (2) that the two kingdoms be incorporated into one; or (3) that they be entirely separated."[1] He subsequently waxed sarcastic upon the subject of "Fœderal Union." "It is true," he said, "the words Fœderal Union are become very fashionable, and may be handsomely fitted to delude unthinking people." He gave no definition of a federal union, but he endeavoured to show, by historical illustration, that it could not prove a permanent bond. And he sought his illustrations, not in Holland or Switzerland, but in the cases of temporary union between Denmark and Sweden in the fifteenth century, and between Spain and Portugal in the sixteenth and seventeenth. Now the union of Denmark with Sweden was brought about by an accident of succession to the two crowns analogous to that which gave England a Scotch king in 1603. The union of Portugal with Spain from 1580 to 1640 was the result of conquest upon a quarrel over the succession to the crown of Portugal. "Fœderal Union," then, clearly meant, in the early years of the eighteenth century, confederation for certain limited purposes, without the uniting bond of a Federal Parliament. Lord Haversham expressed

[1] Parl. Hist., vol. 6, appendix i., col. cxxxviii.

the current English conception of federation when he said: "I would not be understood as if I were against an union. A Fœderal Union, *an union of interest, an union in succession*, is what I shall always be for."[1]

The reason why England could not accept such a solution is manifest. Her prime object in the negotiations was to secure herself against a hostile Scotland in alliance with France. The mere acceptance on paper by Scotland of the Hanoverian succession would have proved but a frail bulwark against that danger if an independent Scots Parliament had been permitted to exist. Such a Parliament would inevitably become a centre for conspiracy and intrigue. No treaty could be made so binding that it could never be broken; no statute could be passed that could not also be repealed. England believed that she was making an enormous sacrifice in surrendering an equality of trade rights to Scotland. She was determined not to pay down the purchase money so long as any risk remained that she might lose her bargain. The extinction of the Scots Parliament was her security. Scotland knew well that she must for ever remain a poverty-stricken agricultural community unless she succeeded in breaking through the ring-fence of English trade monopoly, and to gain this end she sacrificed her independence.

[1] Parl. Hist., vol. 6, c. 563.

The permanent forces, therefore, which would have made for federation rather than incorporation, were overwhelmed by the perturbing force of temporary political necessity. It is worth while noting how transient was their operation. Before the century had closed Scotland had become no less ardent than England in her support of the union of crowns. Fifty years later England and Scotland had so altered their views upon trade questions that the priceless boon of 1707 had come to be looked upon as an intolerable burden. Our ports were opened to all the world. The conditions which had forced the incorporating union upon the two countries had disappeared, while the conditions which make for federation remained.

Neither a "common national feeling" nor a "sense of common interests" produced the Union. It might be more accurately described as a peaceful conquest of Scotland by England. Such relations necessarily engendered bitter sentiments in the weaker nation, and the policy of England did not tend to soften them. When Esau sold his birthright for a mess of pottage, it is probable that he resented continual reminders of the fact; and Scotland, poor and proud, was irritated beyond endurance by a policy which never allowed her to forget her lost independence. The abolition of the Scots Privy Council; the extension of the English law of treason to Scotland; the imposition of the malt tax, contrary to the spirit, if not the letter, of the Act of Union; the insult offered by the House of Lords to the Scots peerage in the person of the Duke of Hamilton, all combined to lash the people into fury. In the debate of 1713, to which reference has already been made, the Scotch representative peers declared that "the end of the Union was the cultivating an amity and friendship between the two nations, but it was so far from having that effect that they were sure that animosities were much greater now than before the Union."[1]

The Union was founded in mutual antipathy and, on the part of Scotland, in hostility. The history of the gradual dying out of that hostility is practically the history of Scotland during the latter half of the eighteenth century. The rebellion of 1715, the tax riots of 1722, the Porteous riot of 1737 and its consequences, and the rebellion of 1745, are only the more prominent landmarks in a survey of Scottish discontent. That discontent culminated in the years following 1745. Andrew Fairservice only expresses the prevailing Scotch opinion of his time in his frequent lamentations over "the sad and sorrowfu' Union."

The severity of England kept pace with Scotland's discontent. The first Scotch Coercion Act[2] was passed in 1716. It inflicted penalties

[1] Parl. Hist., vol. 6, c. 1218.
[2] 2 Geo. I., c. 54.

of fine and imprisonment for carrying arms in the northern and western counties. But its provisions proved ineffectual, and in 1724 a strengthening Act was passed. Any man who failed to surrender his arms in response to a proclamation,[1] which was authorised to be issued, was liable to be condemned to serve in the army beyond seas; a woman could be imprisoned for two years and fined for a similar offence. After the rebellion of 1745, a still more stringent Act was passed. The penalties for men remained much the same, but women, for a second offence, could be transported for seven years.[2] Further coercive measures were applied to the whole of Scotland. No man or boy not in His Majesty's service was permitted to wear the national dress. The penalties were six months' imprisonment for the first offence, and transportation for seven years for the second. Every private school had to be registered, and every master who taught in any such school was compelled to take the oaths of allegiance and abjuration, and to pray for the King by name so often as prayers were offered. The penalties for non-compliance were six months' imprisonment for the first offence, and transportation for life for the second. The parent of any child who was taught in an unregistered school was liable to imprisonment for two years.

---

[1] 11 Geo. I., c. 26.
[2] 19 Geo. II., c. 39.   See also 21 Geo. II., c. 34.

These measures of repression have not been cited for the purpose of condemning them. It is possible that they were justified by the circumstances of the time. They are only called in evidence to prove how untenable is the contention that there was any " common national feeling " or " sense of common interests " pervading the two countries.

When did this national antipathy cease to be a political factor, and what were the agencies which caused its disappearance? It is a fair contention that it had not entirely passed away until the Government was convinced that the middle classes of Scotland might be entrusted with the possession of arms. The first of the annual Acts for embodying the Scotch militia was passed in 1797.[1] A few years before, in 1793, the " fencible men " had been re-organised, but it is evident that they were far from being an efficient force. Attempts had been unsuccessfully made in previous years to obtain powers for the levy of a militia in Scotland. In 1782, when England was engaged in a death-struggle with Spain, France and the United States, and had recently added Holland to the number of her foes, a motion was made in the House of Commons for leave to bring in a bill for that purpose. It was contended on behalf of Scotland that the declaration of war

---

[1] 37 Geo. III., c. 103.

against Holland[1] had exposed her to more immediate danger from invasion than heretofore, and that, unless Parliament took the matter into consideration, the Scots would be compelled to arm themselves in self-defence. It was also contended that the old national feud was dead, and that "no men had proved themselves firmer supporters of the crown than the Scotch." The bill was brought in, but it was dropped in committee.[2] Experience of the Irish volunteers may have made the Government chary lest they should do anything to encourage a movement in Scotland which would have the effect of placing weapons under the control of the populace. It is worthy of note that in the very year in which England was granting untrammelled self-government to Ireland, she had not the courage to trust Scotland with the means of defending herself against invasion. But in that year Government made a concession to Scotch national sentiment by the repeal of those clauses in the Disarmament Act of 1746 which prohibited the use of the national dress.[3] A Scotch militia bill was read a first time and dropped in 1793, the year in which the fencible men were enrolled. It may be assumed, therefore, that at this period statesmen were convinced that if the Scotch were permitted to arm

---

[1] Parl. Hist., vol. 23, c. 14.
[2] Commons' Journals, vol. 38, p. 1048.
[3] 22 Geo. III., c. 63.

a national force, that force would be used for purposes of national defence, and not for purposes of sedition. But the sense of national antipathy had probably become extinct some years before the official mind was convinced of its extinction. The Act of 1784 for the restoration of estates which had been forfeited for treasonable practices, helps to fix the date when authority ceased to dread Scottish discontent. The decade 1780-1790 appears to be indicated with some definiteness as the close of that period of Scotch history which has been termed the period of resistance.

Several causes, which can only be summarised, co-operated to bring about this result. The Scots were slowly convinced that resistance to the new order of things was futile, and they schooled themselves to submit to the inevitable. The drunkard who aspired to call himself King of Great Britain and Ireland was hardly the type of leader to revive waning enthusiasm. Although the office of Secretary of State for Scotland was definitely abolished after "the '45," and although, as we have seen, measures of a severely repressive character were adopted, in other respects a very definite attempt was made to govern Scotland in accordance with Scotch ideas, and to seek the advice of Scotchmen who understood her needs.[1] The policy of purchasing the heritable jurisdic-

[1] Burton: "History of Scotland," vol. 8, p. 502.

tions, which were, under the guise of law, responsible for more lawlessness than should have been possible in a nation pretending to be civilised, advanced the cause of civic order, conciliated the Scots aristocracy and provided them with much-needed funds for the improvement of their estates. It was after 1750 that Scotland began to reap the full benefit of the commercial clauses of the Union; before that date their benefits appear to have been confined chiefly to Glasgow. The new system of agriculture, with which the name of Sir John Sinclair is chiefly associated, was introduced during the latter part of the century, with the result that the value of land and the prosperity of farmers were greatly increased. And lastly, Scotland found herself treated as an integral portion of the kingdom by the enemies of England in the wild world-struggle with which the century closed. She was exposed to their attack, and she had no efficient national force with which to resist a sudden and unexpected assault. She was dependent for protection entirely upon the Government, and a common danger is proverbially a healer of intestine feuds.

But when all these considerations have been taken into account, it is doubtful whether the new sentiment of Scotland was anything deeper than acquiescence in an accomplished fact. Her people were practically voiceless in Parliament until 1832.[1] Her representation was in the hands of a few great families, who found their interest in supporting the Government. Moreover, there was no ground for attributing the growing prosperity of Scotland to the fact that the Union was an incorporating union, because the only causes of that prosperity which can be traced to political conditions, namely, equality of trade and unity in national defence, would also have been secured by a federal union. But it matters little whether we conclude that Scotland merely acquiesced in, or that she cordially approved, the policy of incorporation. Her subsequent dissatisfaction becomes the more remarkable if we admit that her attitude was one of cordial approval.

[1] Oldfield: " Representative History," vol. 6, p. 294.

CHAPTER IX

THE BURDEN OF SCOTLAND (*continued*)

SEVENTY or eighty years elapsed before the result which has been described was finally achieved, and those years were followed by a period of about the same length, during which Scotland had little or no political history. That period has been classified as one of acquiescence in the constitution. It is true that during the last decade of the century Scotland was agitated by political ferment, and prosecutions for sedition were not infrequent. But this agitation was caused by deep-rooted discontent with the policy of Pitt, a discontent which afflicted England no less than Scotland, and also by the unrest which was the consequence of the French Revolution. It does not appear to have been directed against the policy of the Union. The very name of the "British Convention," which assembled at Edinburgh in imitation of the Irish Catholic Convention, negatives the supposition that the movement was hostile to England. The two countries were making common cause against an oligarchy.

Scotland was also violently agitated by the great struggle for reform, a question in which she was even more vitally interested than England. But in this case again her interests were identical with, not opposed to, those of the sister country. The two nations fought the battle shoulder to shoulder, and victory gave Scotland, for the first time, an articulate political voice.

Beyond these two instances the course of Scottish politics was smooth and uneventful until the middle of the present century. The only instance in which national feeling was thoroughly roused was when Government proposed to force the "Small Notes" bill of 1826 upon Scotland. The horrible Scotch £1 note is a national institution, and the proposal to suppress it caused an ebullition of indignation. Sir Walter Scott, who had been ruined by the financial collapse which made the bill necessary, came forward to champion the cause of the greasy currency. The Government eventually bowed before the storm, and confined the operation of the Act to England. The triviality of the grievance and the promptitude with which it was redressed prove that Scotland had, during the earlier half of the century, no very serious complaint against the incorporating union. The period of acquiescence lasted at least until 1850.

But with the advent of the fifties we notice the commencement of a change of opinion. On the 21st of July, 1853, the *Times* expressed itself in the following lugubrious strain, " It is with feelings of great regret that we observe the first symptoms of an agitation which threatens to arise in Scotland, having for its object the resuscitation of the national spirit, and redress of those grievances and inequalities under which, it is alleged, the sister kingdom labours." This lamentation was called forth by the publication of the demands of a recently formed society, called " The National Association for the Vindication of Scottish Rights." The demands of that association were about thirty in number. The most important of these were : (1) The appointment of a Secretary of State for Scotland ; (2) increased parliamentary representation to secure greater attention to Scotch legislation ; (3) a larger share of the national expenditure on charitable institutions, the police force, harbours of refuge, and maintenance of royal palaces ; and (4) the administration of Crown property by a Scotch Board. There were some absurdities in the new programme, such as the demand that when the Royal arms were displayed in Scotland, the Scotch arms should have precedence over those of England. But there was nothing so fantastic as to justify the *Times*[1] in demanding to be informed whether we were " to discard our comfortable clothing, paint our bodies with blue

[1] July 7th, 1853.

woad, and run howling about Hampstead Heath," because Scotland showed signs of dissatisfaction.

The new movement received public sanction and support at a public meeting which was held at Edinburgh in the following November; a meeting which was said to have been the largest and most influential which had ever been called together in Scotland. Five resolutions were passed unanimously. Four of them echoed the complaints which have been already enumerated; the fifth pledged the meeting to support the National Association. The complaints were subsequently embodied in a petition to the House of Lords, and Lord Eglinton, who had acted as chairman of the Edinburgh meeting, presented it, and moved for an address to the Crown praying that its contents might be taken into consideration.[1] The motion was, of course, negatived.

The significance of the dates at which these demands were made must not be overlooked. They came into prominence precisely in that decade (1851-60) in which, as we have already ascertained, the work demanded of Parliament was greater than Parliament was able to transact, and in which, consequently, the interests of the minor States were more liable to be sacrificed. It should be noticed also that in the previous decade, during which, as we have seen, Parliament was approaching perilously near to con-

---

[1] Hansard, vol. 132, c. 496.

gestion, both the average and percentage of Scotch legislation had fallen considerably. The national movement, therefore, was no bolt from the blue, no sudden ebullition of popular and transient political passion. It is traceable to very clearly defined causes which have since continued to operate with ever-increasing force. If the quiescence of the period, which lasted from about 1780 to 1850, can justly be traced to the development of "a sense of common interests," or "a common national feeling," then the renewal of agitation after the latter date must be attributed to a conviction on the part of the Scotch people that that feeling and those interests were not after all so strong and so inseparable as they had imagined.

It must be noticed that these proceedings at Edinburgh, which contained the germ of an agitation which has since continued to grow vigorously, were commenced with a two-fold object. The promoters of the movement desired to ensure: (1) Greater security that Scotch State legislation should be efficient; and (2) the separate administration of Scotch State affairs. In 1854 the former demand did not go beyond a claim for an increase of the Scotch representation in the Imperial Parliament. Since that date it has gradually developed into a demand for local self-government, notwithstanding the fact that the representation of Scotland has been increased by nineteen members. The claim for separate administration has been absolutely conceded. For the sake of clearness, the history of the two subjects will be sketched separately.

The demand for a Scotch minister, which had been ridiculed in the House of Lords in 1854, was repeated in the House of Commons four years later. In 1858 a Scotch member, Mr. Baxter, moved for the appointment of a Scotch Under-Secretary of State.[1] The chief ground of the motion was that, on account of the great recent growth of public business, it was impossible for the Home Secretary, overwhelmed as he was with English work, and for the Lord Advocate, "who combined in his own proper person all the abolished offices of State which formerly existed in Scotland," and who, in addition, was always an advocate with a large Scotch practice, to transact the whole of the Scotch business which was cast upon them. Scotch administration was, consequently, habitually neglected, and Scotch bills were constantly postponed.

The motion was lost by a majority of 127.[2] It is remarkable that during the whole debate scarcely a member ventured to assert that the Scotch grievance was purely imaginary, or that there was any gradual amalgamation of Scotch and English administration in progress which

[1] Hansard, vol. 150, c. 2118.
[2] Ayes 47, Noes 174.

would eventually obviate any necessity for constitutional change. It is remarkable also that some of the Scotch members opposed the motion, not on account of its tendency to undermine the Union, but because they feared lest the appointment of a Scotch Secretary should be prejudicial to the Scotch nationality. The Lord Advocate was, they said, of necessity frequently in Edinburgh, and was brought directly into touch with Scotch opinion. A Scotch Secretaryship would only tend towards further centralisation of Scotch business in London.

The large majority against Mr. Baxter's motion was discouraging. The question was not raised again until 1864, and then upon a more general issue. Sir James Fergusson moved for a select committee to inquire "how far the number of members of the administration charged with the conduct of the affairs of Scotland, and having seats in Parliament, is commensurate with the needs of that part of the United Kingdom."[1] But the object which was sought and the arguments which were used were the same. The burden of complaint was that Scotch administration was scamped and Scotch legislation was neglected. One Scotch member went so far as to declare that "fish are certainly well taken care of in Scotland, but Scotchmen are not so well attended to."[2] After two unsuccessful

[1] Hansard, vol. 175, c. 1167.
[2] Ib., vol. 175, c. 1192.

attempts to count out the House, the motion was withdrawn. The subject was revived in 1867 and 1869,[1] but without result. The consequence of this continued neglect of a demand which Scotch members were constantly pressing upon the Government, was the great debate of 1872, in which the proposal for local self-government was first brought before the House of Commons for discussion.[2] The demand for a Scotch minister was repeated in 1877,[3] and the debate contains indications that the sentiment in favour of a State legislature for dealing with purely State questions had gained considerable ground.

It had become evident that the wishes of Scotland could no longer be successfully resisted. In the last-mentioned debate a Scotch member had stated that "the feeling in Scotland was so strong that when Scotch members went down to their constituents they found that the two great subjects of interest were the Eastern question and the neglect of Scotch business." The Government introduced a bill for creating an Under-Secretary for Scotland;[4] but this proposal, which had been made by Scotch representatives twenty years before, now failed to satisfy them. They demanded a full-blown

[1] Hansard, vol. 186, c. 397; vol. 198, c. 1296.
[2] See *post*, p. 161.
[3] Hansard, vol. 232, c. 929.
[4] *Ib.*, vol. 240, c. 821.

Secretary with Cabinet rank. The bill failed to receive any general support, and it was withdrawn after the second reading.

After that failure, legislation was not again attempted until 1883. In that year Government introduced the " Local Government Board (Scotland) Bill."[1] The proposal was that a Scotch Local Government Board should be created, with a President at its head who should be capable of sitting in the House of Commons. This was by no means what the Scotch members desired. They had been pressing for some years for a Scotch Secretary of State with a seat in the Cabinet. One of them declared that the bill, "in its disregard of the expectations and demands of the Scotch people, and in its inadequacy to meet the circumstances of the case, was essentially English." They supported it coldly, on the ground that it was a step, although a short one, in the right direction. The bill passed the Commons, but it was rejected in the House of Lords, ostensibly because of the lateness of the session, but really, as the mover of the rejection declared, because "it was the commencement of a wholly new line of policy in regard to the government of Scotland," and "he thought they should not lightly depart from what had hitherto been the policy of Parliament, namely, to unite the governments of England

[1] Hansard, vol. 280, c. 1984.

and Scotland as far as possible, and not to separate them."[1]

But the inexorable compulsion of fact and of opinion was forcing Parliament to depart from that policy. During the recess a great meeting was held in Edinburgh to demand the appointment of a Scotch Secretary. In 1884 the Government frankly recognised the trend of Scottish opinion, and introduced a bill for that purpose in the House of Lords.[2] The Scotch had thus gained a great step towards the attainment of their ideal, but they were dissatisfied with the limitations which were imposed by the bill upon the activity of the Scotch Secretary. The Government declined to transfer to that official the administration of matters relating to law and justice, and to elementary education. An amendment was moved to include the former subject, and although the Government opposed it, they did not venture to divide against it.[3] The third reading was reached soon after the rejection of the Franchise Bill, and on the very day when the Prime Minister was proposing in the House of Commons to wind up business as speedily as possible with a view to an early autumn session. The bill was therefore dropped.[4]

In 1885 a new bill was brought in.[5] It gave

[1] Lord Balfour. Hansard, vol. 283, c. 1468.
[2] Hansard, vol. 287, c. 1664.
[3] Ib., vol. 289, c. 1339.
[4] Ib., vol. 290, c. 650.
[5] Ib., vol. 298, c. 567.

the Scotch Secretary control of public elementary education, but it omitted the amendment relating to law and justice which had been forced upon Government in the previous year. The bill passed the Lords, and, after a stiff fight upon the inclusion of education, it was agreed to by the House of Commons.[1]

The business transferred to the newly-created Secretary of State for Scotland affected a vast number of subjects. The administration of most local affairs, from poor law and public health to vaccination and burial grounds, was handed over to him, but within two years it was found that the transfer had not been sufficiently complete. An amending Act was passed in 1887,[2] which invested the Scotch Secretary not only with the administration of all matters pertaining to law and justice, except the power to advise upon the exercise of the prerogative of mercy, but also all powers then vested in any Secretary of State, except in relation to six specified subjects. So complete was the transfer that it became necessary in 1889 to pass a short Act declaring that the functions of the Secretary for War were not to be deemed to be vested in the Scotch Secretary.[3]

The changes which have been thus shortly described were in fact an administrative revolu-

---

[1] 48 and 49 Vict., c. 61.
[2] 50 and 51 Vict., c. 52.
[3] 52 and 53 Vict., c. 16.

tion. It must surely be a source of some surprise to believers in the doctrine that " the sense of common interests " is too strong in England and Scotland to allow of " that combination of union and separation " which is the foundation of federalism, to find that within the last forty years the Scotch have demanded and obtained the separate administration of a large number of matters, most of which had for more than a hundred years previously been dealt with by one set of officials for both countries "in a spirit of unity." Lord Salisbury, in 1884, pointed out that the proposed change was a return to the policy which had been abandoned in 1745.[1] The statement is true and significant. It proves the permanence in Scotland of that tendency to assert separate State rights which makes for federalism, but which was overwhelmed at the time of the Union by transient political exigencies. The inextinguishable vitality of that tendency may be illustrated by quotations from speeches by two statesmen, the latter of which was uttered exactly 180 years after the earlier. In 1707 Lord Haversham said that it was a question " whether two nations, independent in their sovereignties, that have their distinct laws and interests, and, what I cannot forget, their different forms of worship, church government, and order, shall be united into one kingdom."[2] The

[1] Hansard, vol. 283, c. 1473.
[2] Parl. Hist., vol. 6, c. 563.

Marquess of Lothian, when moving the second reading of the Amendment Bill of 1887, said: "After the long period of intimate union between England and Scotland, which has lasted now nearly two hundred years, people are apt to forget how entirely distinctive and different the administration of Scotland is from that of England. There is almost no point of resemblance. There are different forms of religion and different social forms affecting every portion of Scotland. There is a different code of education—an entirely different code of education—and different systems of agriculture. There are also different systems affecting the law of lunacy and parochial laws, and almost every other department."[1] The statesman of the present day endorses and expands the declaration of the statesman of 1707. He has to admit, not only that the interests which were separate at the time of the Union have shown no sign of amalgamation, but also that those functions of government which are of more recent creation have, from sheer force of circumstances, developed a system of individuality, not of unity.

This portion of the investigation into the relation of Scotland to the Union may be fitly closed by calling attention to the marvellous success which has crowned the efforts of the Scotch to secure separate administra-

[1] Hansard, vol. 318, c. 687.

tion. It is an apt illustration of their keen political instinct; and it is an object lesson in political conduct. The Scotch came to the definite conclusion in 1853 that their affairs would never be efficiently conducted until they secured, among other reforms, the appointment of a Secretary of State for the control of Scotch administration. Their proposal was at the outset denounced and decried. Its advocates were treated as if they were irresponsible and not altogether harmless lunatics. Both the great parties in the State set their faces against it. It was branded as an attempt to tamper with the sacred Union. But the Scotch representatives had made up their minds, and they never swerved in the prosecution of their object. The result was that within thirty-three years from the time when the proposal was first made, they had received, through the combined action of both the great parties in the State, one of the chief of those demands which, at the outset, the *Times* had declared would tend to reduce us as a nation to a state of primeval savagery.

By what methods was this success achieved? Dogged persistence, a clear perception of the end in view, a consistent moderation in the statement of the case, and a fixed determination to avoid offence to the susceptibilities and prejudices of those whose co-operation must of necessity be secured, were important factors in the campaign.

But the victory was more especially due to the fact that Scotch members always accepted such portion of their policy as the Government of the day was prepared to concede. None of the bills and Acts which have been described were entirely satisfactory to them. But they knew that in England no policy can be effected at one stroke, and they wisely contented themselves with such instalments as they could, for the time being, obtain. They knew that half a political loaf was better than no political bread. If they had pursued the opposite course, and had opposed the bills because they did not fully realise their ideal, it is doubtful whether a Secretary for Scotland would be sitting in the Cabinet at the present moment. By constant exercise of those political virtues which I have endeavoured to describe, the Scotch have effected a revolution silently and without disturbance. The moral is clear: it is foreign to my purpose to attempt the application of it.

CHAPTER X

THE BURDEN OF SCOTLAND (*continued*)

IN the year 1886 the Scotch had secured the two main political reforms which the recrudescence of nationalism in 1853 had led them to demand. They had their own Secretary of State, and their representation had been increased. Were the Scotch content with their victory? The records of Parliament return a conclusive negative answer to the question. The reason for this absence of content was two-fold. In the first place, the creation of a Secretary of State for Scotland only tended to accentuate another constitutional anomaly. The theory is that ministers derive their power from the support of the majority of the elected representatives of the nation. When that support is withdrawn, the administration ceases to exist; when a motion equivalent to a vote of no confidence in any particular minister is carried, that minister is bound to resign. But it happened that for six years after the creation of the Scotch Secretary a Government was in power which did not receive the political support of the majority of

Scotch members. At any moment during those six years, if the question of "no confidence" in the Secretary for Scotland had been submitted to the Scotch members only, it would have been carried by a large majority. He was kept in power by the reserve force of English members, who outvoted the Scotch. The Scotch found that they had acquired the form of national administration without the power thereof. They had obtained their Scotch minister, but they were quite unable to control his administrative acts.

A second cause of discontent was that they had discovered that an increase of their representation, although it might palliate, could not cure the evils from which they suffered. The larger the numerical force of a State representation the greater is the chance that the measures for that State will meet with success. But increased representation can do nothing towards making time for the consideration of measures when Parliament is overtaxed with work. Neither could a Scotch Secretary, however great his adroitness and tact, do much to facilitate legislation in a congested assembly.[1] To expect it would be the expectation of a miracle. These facts were clearly perceived by

[1] A minor cause of complaint was that for a considerable period the Secretary for Scotland was a peer, and was on that account useless for the purpose of promoting Scottish interests in the House of Commons.

the Scotch members. Before they had succeeded in either their demand for a Scotch Secretary or for increased representation, many of them had recognised that the only true remedy for the parliamentary paralysis which had been caused by over-pressure of States work, was to be found in devolution of State affairs.

This variation of the Scotch demand was expressed in a very tentative way in 1872. In that year Sir David Wedderburn moved "that a select committee be appointed to inquire and report upon the best means of promoting the dispatch of Scotch parliamentary business."[1] The speech in which he introduced his subject is a model of lucidity and moderation. "The subject which I venture to lay before the attention of the House," he said, "is a limited branch of one which must ere long attract the attention of Parliament, namely, whether it is possible in any way to relieve Parliament in some measure of the accumulated weight of legislative work which almost threatens to overwhelm it." After explaining why the case of Scotland was a peculiarly favourable one for dispassionate consideration, he continued: "I know that in bringing this subject forward I may be told that I am attempting Home Rule for Scotland. Before either admitting or denying the truth

[1] Hansard, vol. 209, c. 1853.

of the assertion I would ask exactly what is implied in the term 'Home Rule'?" And he proceeded to draw the distinction between local self-government and separation, which might be thought superfluous were it not for the fact that the sillier sort of journalists of the present day persist in confounding them.

He then went on to point out one of the weaknesses of our constitution which we have already considered. "It is because," he said, "the very centralisation of our present system seems to menace in various parts of the Empire the integrity of our Empire, that I now would call the attention of the House to its evil effects in a part of the country where no such danger can be at all apprehended."

"In the case of Scotland we have a distinct system of laws and customs and of traditions, and it appears to me that if these laws and customs are to be remodelled so as to suit the growing wants of the community, this will be best done by the people themselves through their representatives, with as little interference as may be on the part of those who are not familiar with the particular laws, customs and institutions."

The chief defects which the speaker enumerated as adversely influencing the business of Scotland were three in number. The first was the non-inclusion of any official representative of Scotland in the Cabinet. This defect, as we have seen, has been remedied. The second was that Scotch members were liable to be outvoted on purely Scotch questions by representatives of the other States. He did not lay any very great stress upon this point. "It is only," he said, "when a question or a bill intended to apply to Scotland exclusively appears prospectively to affect the law of England that we find English members—the bulk of this House—voting against the clearly-expressed will of the Scotch representatives." In later years Scotch members have told a different tale. In advocating local self-government for Scotland they have cited other cases in which England has deliberately overridden Scotch opinion.[1] But even as it stands the charge is a serious one. The English members are accused of dealing with Scotch questions, not upon the basis of Scotland's needs or wishes, but upon the basis of how the proposed legislation will affect England. It is precisely the evil which we found must result from the constitutional system which we have adopted.

The third defect was that there was no parliamentary time to discuss Scotch measures in detail, and to pass those measures which were necessary. "To legislate for a country of three million people involves," the speaker said, "nearly as many difficulties as to legislate for thirty million."

[1] See Hansard, vol. 341, c. 677 *et seq.*

"The problem before us is that we have to legislate separately for an independent province in our imperial assembly, and the solution of the problem, as at present worked out, is that it is impossible to obtain from this imperial assembly time to discuss details which are unfamiliar to the great bulk of the assembly, in which they feel no direct interest and for which they have no direct responsibility." The consequences were that Scotch independent members had not the remotest chance of carrying a bill. The Scotch measures which had recommended themselves to the Scotch constituencies at the General Election four years previously had not even been touched. If Scotch business could be settled informally by Scotch members outside the House, and discussion were avoided, it might by chance be passed; otherwise it was always introduced so late in the session that it was certain to be dropped. Scotland was becoming more and more convinced that her interests were neglected. "Oh," exclaimed the speaker, "that we were like Man!"

The proposed reforms were curiously inadequate to remedy the defects which had been enumerated. They are characteristic of the cautious and tentative manner in which the Scotch were at first prepared to proceed. They were (1) to relieve Parliament of all private legislation, and (2) to treat Scotch State legislation in the same manner as local and personal bills. " When any measure has received the sanction of this House as not being contrary to the policy or the constitution of the Empire, why should not the details of that measure be referred to a committee of those who are acquainted with the details, who are interested directly in them, and who are directly responsible to their constituents for the proper management and carrying out of those details." The idea was that when the Imperial Parliament had sanctioned the principle of a "State" bill, the settlement of the details of that bill should be left to the members of that State. If such a scheme were practicable it would do away with many of the evils inherent in our present system. The motion met with the usual fate which always impends over debates upon Scottish questions: it was counted out.

I have allowed Sir David Wedderburn to state his case, as far as possible, in his own words. It will be seen that although his premises pointed very distinctly to federation, he refrained from drawing that conclusion from them. He knew that neither the House nor the nation was prepared for such a policy. He went just so far along the road towards his goal as he thought his hearers could be enticed. The wisdom of this course was made clear by the speech delivered by Mr. Gladstone. " The mind of the House was, he feared, not yet ripe for any vigorous and comprehensive effort for the solution of those difficulties. In this country it commonly happened that people groaned a good deal over the inconveniences which oppressed them before they could see their way to any mode of escape. It might be that they might find a remedy for the great evil they laboured under." That statement precisely represented the facts of the case. The nation had been groaning over the paralysis of Parliament for about twenty years, and was going to continue the performance for as many years more before it saw its way "to any mode of escape," and then the vision was but dim and distorted. But the curious fact is that Mr. Gladstone had not at that time perceived the remedy. He said that "he should regard with considerable jealousy suggestions which tended to a division of the interests of the three kingdoms. He was not at all shocked at the proposal of an alteration in the mere machinery of the House, but although this pressure was in some degree of a temporary nature, it might prove to be to a considerable extent permanent in its character, and might require very considerable measures for its relief. But he hoped that those measures would not under any circumstances tend in the remotest degree to a separation of interests as between the three countries. . . . He owned that he should object to the handing over under any circumstances, to the representatives of one country exclusively, the manipulation of measures brought before the House having reference to the interests of that country." That was in 1872. In 1886 Mr. Gladstone introduced into Parliament a bill for granting local self-government to Ireland.

The subject was approached in a more combative spirit in 1877. Sir George Campbell called attention "to the extreme neglect of Scotch business in the session of 1876," and suggested "the necessity of relieving the pressure which is now felt in this House, and improving the arrangements for the conduct of business."[1] The actual demands were similar to those made in 1872, but from the tone of the debate it was evident that Scotch members were smarting under a sense of their want of power to promote Scotch business. The proposal was not carried to a division.

The subject was not renewed in formal debate for ten years, but the pages of Hansard bear evidence, mainly in the form of questions addressed to ministers, of the continued neglect of Scotch business and of the increasing irritation of Scotch members.[2] It must be remembered that in the

[1] Hansard, vol. 232, c. 929.
[2] Hansard, vol. 237, c. 379; vol. 240, c. 25; vol. 248, c. 632; vol. 255, c. 1221; vol. 264, c. 370; vol. 265, c. 818; vol. 269, c. 1790; vol. 270, c. 1272; vol. 272, c. 720; vol. 273, c. 1674; vol. 277, c. 1504; vol. 279, c. 777, 1104, 1919; vol. 280, c. 1424, 1713; vol. 281, c. 51, 1527; vol. 282, c. 788; vol. 283, c. 69; vol. 291, c. 1188; vol. 293, c. 526, 1853; vol. 300, c. 242.

interim the Scotch had secured their Secretary of State for Scotland and their increased representation. It was natural that they should remain quiescent awhile to see how the new system worked. The circumstances were, as we have seen, unfortunate for the success of the experiment. For six years the Scotch were governed by their minority, and the Scotch Secretary represented the wishes of the minority. Moreover, for a great part of that period the Scotch Secretary sat in the House of Lords, and was, therefore, not in close touch with Scotch members, or easily accessible to them. In 1887 the Scotch discovered that not only the reforms which they had secured, but also those which they had hitherto advocated, were insufficient to meet the needs of the case. For the first time they boldly declared in favour of some scheme of federation, in an amendment to the Address.

The terms of the amendment were: "Humbly to submit to Her Majesty that the affairs of the realm have outgrown the capacity of this House, and humbly to pray of Her Majesty to invite Her Majesty's ministers to consider and submit to Parliament measures whereby great part of the special affairs of Scotland and of other parts of Great Britain may be relegated to bodies representing the several parts of the kingdom, and the excessive burden on this House may be relieved."[1]

[1] Hansard, vol. 310, c. 1474.

A clumsier resolution was never drawn; but the object of its promoters nevertheless remains clear. It represents with some accuracy their state of mind upon the subject. They felt acutely enough the pinch of the inconvenience of the present system, but they had never attempted to track that inconvenience down to its ultimate cause, and they were consequently incapable of accurately defining the nature of the remedy. This condition of mind was reflected in the speeches which were delivered in support of the amendment. The mover had no definite plan to suggest, and it is evident that he had never applied himself to the consideration of the nature of a federal union. The fact that he was prepared to consider the claims of London to be "a part of Great Britain" which was entitled to a local legislature is sufficient to prove this. With regard to Scotland the only conclusion upon which he was clear was that the Irish Home Rule scheme was not what the Scotch wanted. But in this respect he was flatly contradicted by the next speaker. Such weakness of perception and lack of unity in purpose delivered the supporters of the amendment into the hands of their enemies, and the amendment was dropped after a short debate.

In 1889 the conception of what was desired had become much clearer and more definite. The question was raised by independent motion in the following terms: "That, in the opinion of this House, it is desirable that arrangements be made for giving to the people of Scotland, by their representatives in a national Parliament, the management and control of Scottish affairs."[1] The mover in this case knew exactly what he wanted. He disclaimed all idea of separation. "All I want," he said, "is that we should keep all the benefits we have under the Union without any of its disadvantages, and I think we can attain this without affecting the Union in any way whatever." He laid great stress upon the almost culpable neglect of Scotch State legislation in the Imperial Parliament, and upon the way in which Scotch opinion was outvoted by English and Irish representatives when Scottish questions were under discussion. The only remedy for this state of things was to be found in devolution upon the lines of nationality. The speaker's scheme was to create national assemblies for each of the three kingdoms, reserving a veto in the Imperial Parliament in case they should trench upon imperial affairs. And, in addition to the State Assembly, there must of necessity be a State Executive. For Scotland, the speaker said that the Executive would consist of the Scotch Secretary of State and the heads of three departments—*i.e.*, the Board of Supervision, the Board of Trade and Agriculture and the Education Board.

[1] Hansard, vol. 335, c. 68.

There can be no mistake about the issue raised in these terms, and Scotch members have since that date practically adhered to them. In every session from 1889 to 1895 the question has been raised and debated, sometimes on the purely Scotch aspect of the case, but more frequently upon the broader basis of local self-government for each of the three kingdoms.[1] It would be wearisome to attempt to wade through all these discussions, more especially as they are merely repetitions, in other forms of words, of the arguments which we have already considered. The case of Scotland for local self-government as stated in all these debates, may be shortly summed up. First, the laws, and consequently the administration of Scotland are " entirely distinct and different " from those of the rest of the United Kingdom, and must perforce be dealt with separately. Secondly, these distinct and separate questions are submitted to the judgment of a majority which is unacquainted with their details and which is incapable of properly understanding their bearings. Thirdly, that on account of the over-pressure upon Parliament, Scotch bills are systematically neglected ; measures of first-class importance are introduced year after year and then dropped ; those which are passed are forced through the House without adequate

---

[1] Hansard, vol. 341, c. 677 (1890); vol. 351, c. 440 (1891). 4th Series, vol. 3, c. 1684 (1892); vol. 13, c. 1828 (1893); vol. 22, c. 1287 (1894); vol. 32, c. 525 (1895).

discussion and at the fag end of the session, with the result that they often fail of their intended purpose; and lastly that, under certain conditions, namely, when the majority in Parliament is not of the same complexion as the Scotch majority, measures are forced upon the Scotch which are not in accordance with their wishes.

The burden of Scotland, then, is that while her political relations with the rest of the United Kingdom entirely correspond with those which are supposed to require a federal system of government, she has been forced into an incorporating union for which there is no present political need. We have seen that these political relations existed at the time of the Union, but that their natural tendency towards some form of federation was destroyed by forces of mutual distrust. Those forces have long since disappeared, while the line of demarcation between the separate State interests of the two nations has been intensified, not obliterated. Then, after a period of acquiescence in the incorporating union — a period quite long enough to enable Scotland to form a just judgment upon the political expediency of absolute incorporation — we observe a sudden revival of the demand for greater national control of national affairs. It breaks forth like an eruption, from no apparent cause; but when the matter is probed deeper we find that it breaks forth precisely at the time when Parliament has become incapable of transacting all the business demanded of it, and when consequently the interests of the least numerously represented nation began to suffer more severely. Since its inception the demand has expanded and defined itself, until for seven years federation has been the settled policy of the majority of Scotch members — the only method by which, in their opinion, the burden of Scotland can be removed.

CHAPTER XI

THE BURDEN OF IRELAND

WE have seen that England, the "predominant partner" in the constitution, shows at times a marked dissatisfaction with the manner in which that constitution works, and that this dissatisfaction arises at those periods when the total parliamentary majority is not of the same political complexion as the majority of English representatives. We have also seen that Scotland, after passing through a preliminary stage of resistance to the incorporating union, and then through a period of acquiescence in it, has, during the last forty years, developed a feeling of dissatisfaction with its working, notwithstanding the fact that she has achieved, by strictly constitutional methods, a political reform which at any rate tends towards the realisation of the federal idea, and which, it was hoped, would satisfy her national aspirations. We must now turn our attention to the case of Ireland.

It was necessary to deal with England and Scotland before approaching Ireland, because the complaints of those two nations can be investigated without arousing political animus to any great extent. It will have been noticed that the acknowledged disadvantage under which England labours is one which is chiefly insisted upon by one of the great political parties in the State, while the complaint of Scotland meets with more general sympathy from the other. But neither party has yet recognised that both England and Scotland are suffering from effects which are in reality due to the same cause. Down to the present point, therefore, it is to be hoped that our investigation has been carried on from a national, and not from the party standpoint, and that the prejudice which arises from the political bias has not been roused into activity.

It is my wish, and it shall be my endeavour, to treat the case of Ireland in the same spirit. But in the very core of it lie brooding the political passions of centuries. A conviction has corroded itself into the heart of Ireland that England is permanently unjust and tyrannical; that having the giant's strength, she has used and will use it like a giant, unscrupulously. England, on the other hand, cannot altogether expel the belief that Ireland is unreasonable and impracticable; that, under the guise of a struggle for Home Rule, she is endeavouring to establish a total independence of England. The sense of a common interest and of a common nationality is in abeyance. Each believes that the realisation of the hopes of the one would be destructive of the interests of the other. The consequence is that it seems impossible for any man who inquires into the subject to put pen to paper unless the virus of political partizanship infects the ink with which he writes. The exponent of Ireland's wrongs only succeeds in inflaming English prejudice; the exponent of England's difficulties makes the hatred of Ireland more bitter; and the pity of it is that on both sides there are not a few who are proud of the mischief thus wrought, and who deem their action patriotic.

It is not my intention to risk incurring the same condemnation by any attempt to trace the history of Irish discontent, and of the Irish demand for local self-government. It was expedient to take that course with regard to Scotland because the Scotch movement has been so quiet and constitutional that it has failed to find a place upon the pages of accepted history. It was therefore necessary to show that the political tendencies which were disclosed by an analysis of legislation and of discussion were producing their inevitable results. But no such burden is cast upon us in the case of Ireland. Her discontent is patent, and her demand for local self-government is permanent. No one will dispute the existence of either. The only points into which we need inquire are, first, how it is that Ireland has never, like Scotland, passed through any period of acquiescence in the incorporating union to another of constitutional dissatisfaction; and, second, whether, assuming for the moment that the demands of Scotland can be safely conceded, there is any reason which should prevent the local self-government for which she asks being also granted to Ireland.

With regard to the first proposition, the lack of any acquiescence by Ireland, even of a temporary character, may be traced not so much to the terms of the Union as to the pre-Union conditions of that State. Scotland before her union with England was practically, except as regarded foreign policy, independent of the English Parliament. That Parliament could not legislate for Scotland. It could regulate Scotch trade with England by the imposition of duties; it could prohibit Scotch trade with English colonies, and thus affect very adversely Scotch agricultural and commercial interests; but it could interfere no further. The Scotch Parliament was uncontrolled in its power to legislate for Scotch agriculture and commerce. It could retaliate upon England with hostile tariffs, and it could regulate without hindrance the laws relating to land. But the case of Ireland was altogether different. The Irish Parliament could pass no law which had not previously been approved by the British

Privy Council, or (after 1782) had been sealed with the Great Seal of Great Britain. Until 1782 England asserted legislative and administrative rights over Ireland. She could not only impose hostile tariffs upon Irish products, but she could also regulate the internal trade of Ireland and her trade with foreign countries. She could dictate the terms upon which Irish land should be held and enjoyed. The Irish Parliament was, in fact, merely the mouthpiece of the English interest.

We have seen that it was the fixed conviction of England, at the time of the union with Scotland, that the commercial prosperity of one nation of necessity implied the commercial depression of the other. She sacrificed that conviction in the case of Scotland to secure herself against a great national danger which might have threatened her very existence. But in the period between the Restoration and the union with Scotland she employed the tremendous power which she wielded over Ireland to give effect to that commercial doctrine in her own favour. Ireland possessed the finest grazing land in the three kingdoms. English landlords, fearing her competition, obtained an absolute prohibition of the importation into England from Ireland of all live and dead stock and dairy produce.[1] In days of slow water transit the prohibition of Ireland's trade in her

---

[1] 18 and 19 Car. II., c. 2; 32 Car. II., c. 2.

chief staple—which was to a great extent perishable—with her nearest neighbour was a blow delivered at her heart. But the door of salvation seemed still open to her. The pasture lands, which would feed the cattle which she might not sell to England, would feed sheep. Irish wool was esteemed the finest in the world. She was forbidden to export it in the raw condition, but no law prevented her from working it herself and exporting the manufactured article, except the Navigation Acts, which prohibited her trade with the Colonies. The woollen manufacture developed rapidly, industrial settlements dotted the land, and Ireland was for a short time threatened with actual prosperity. But England would not suffer it. The commercial classes, who had risen to power after the Revolution, took alarm. The Irish Parliament was compelled to impose export duties on Irish woollen goods.[1] But even this harsh measure did not satisfy England. In 1699 the English Parliament passed an Act which absolutely prohibited the export of woollens from Ireland.[2] The consequence was that the Irish woollen manufacture died down even more rapidly than it had sprung up, and ruined cottages only remained to mark the track of the English spoiler.

Ireland was thus reduced to this position. Being a country especially adapted for raising

---

[1] Irish Statutes, 10 Will. III., c. 5.
[2] 11 Will. III., c. 13, s. 9.

live stock, she was prohibited from dealing in that stock or its produce in her nearest market, and the one manufacture which could be carried on with conspicuous success in all parts of the island was excluded from the markets of the world.

The navigation laws themselves were a cruel blow to Ireland's commercial prosperity. Her position gave her immense natural advantages for the prosecution of the colonial trade, had she been left free to avail herself of them. England's colonies at the time consisted in the American plantations and a few West Indian islands. Ireland was some days nearer to them than England, and she possessed excellent harbours. But a series of Acts which provided that goods could only be exported to the colonies in ships which were English built and English manned, and that no colonial goods could be imported except through England, crushed the Irish shipping interest, and rendered a colonial market for her produce impossible.[1]

Such were the commercial conditions of Ireland at the time when the union with Scotland was effected, and when the latter country was admitted to the benefits of commercial equality with England. Scotland was, as we

---

[1] 15 Car. II., c. 7; 22 and 23 Car. II., c. 26; 7 and 8 Will. III., c. 22.

have seen, slow to reap the full advantage of her admission into the customs union, but during the first half of the eighteenth century she was laying the foundations of the commercial prosperity which came to her before the century had closed. Even during the earlier period Glasgow had risen from a fishing village to be a thriving port with a considerable American trade—a blessing which might have been conferred upon many an Irish sea-board hamlet, far more favourably situated, had it not been for the commercial restrictions. While this constructive process was silently proceeding in Scotland, the destructive process was continued in Ireland to such an extent that she was incapable of taking advantage of her freedom when her shackles were struck off. England was perpetually preaching to Ireland by her actions the truth of Romeo's warning to the apothecary: "This world is not thy friend, nor this world's law." The only difference was that England did not seek the poison, she offered it. Ireland was taught that she must live a life of exclusion from the brotherhood of nations; that the food which she raised she must consume; that the raiment which she wrought she must wear. What wonder that her people became destitute of energy and enterprise. They could not have been otherwise. What wonder that they should sigh for independence as a prisoner sighs for liberty. It is the natural consequence of the endeavour to govern people by laws to which they have never assented, and which offend the first principles of justice.

This policy of repressing all natural commercial expansion in the directions indicated by the position and by the natural resources of the nation was steadily pursued during the greater part of the eighteenth century, and it was pursued by methods which were conspicuously unjust and offensive. It is often said that the evils consequent upon the destruction of the woollen trade were tempered by the toleration by England of the Irish linen and hempen trade. The amelioration was but small. A manufacture, already prosperous, which could be conveniently carried on in all parts of the country, was destroyed, and another, quite in its infancy, which could be established with success in certain portions of Ireland only, was to be fostered. Linen and hemp manufactures were to be admitted into England, but not into the colonies, free. England pledged herself to protect Irish linen and hemp manufactures at the price of the abandonment of the Irish woollen trade. The act of destruction was completed in 1699. In 1705 England, having secured the wool monopoly, began to rue her generosity. The better class of Irish linen goods, the dyed and the striped, were competing with her own in the market, so she promptly, in defiance of the understanding of a few years before, imposed a prohibitive duty of 30 per cent. upon the importation of these goods into England, and relaxed the navigation laws so as to allow Ireland to export her coarser products, the white and brown linens, to the colonies.[1] Ireland had been actually achieving some small success in the only branch of manufacture in which she was free to engage, and that success had to be checked at all hazards. Later in the century the coarser linens were also subjected to a duty, with the result that the skilled artisans of Ulster emigrated to America by thousands, to take revenge upon their persecutors in the War of Independence. The hempen manufacture fared no better. It was destroyed by the imposition of a duty on sailcloth.

Such was the policy of England towards Ireland in regard to textile manufactures. She was freed from any serious Irish competition in the metal trades because Ireland had no coalfields. The consequence was that Ireland was reduced to the condition of a purely agricultural country, hampered, as we have seen, by irritating restrictions. What then was the policy of England towards Irish agriculture during the eighteenth century? The legislation of the seventeenth century excluded Ireland from

---

[1] Lecky's "History of England," vol. 2, p. 212.

all trade in agricultural produce with England and the colonies. The result was that France was practically her only customer, and Ireland's trade with France, except in contraband wool, was exceedingly small. In consequence of this limitation Ireland passed through a long period of chronic famine and depopulation.[1] It may seem paradoxical to assert that a nation which is bound to consume its own produce is bound to be reduced to starvation, but it is a fact. In such a country there is no incentive to production. The slightest over-production means a fall in prices; the slightest under-production means famine. The people are driven to the hazardous task of producing the exact proportion of food which will support existence; a bad season upsets the calculation and brings the wolf to the door. The tendency of such conditions is to make each man crave just so much ground as will raise food sufficient to support him and his family. They create the "earth-hunger," and the earth-hunger incites the cupidity of the landowner. It was just at the time of Ireland's greatest suffering that the landlords, most of whom were aliens or absentees, took advantage of this melancholy and desperate craving.[2] The first great rent-raising took place. The landlord perceived that the tenant must take his holding at the landlord's

---

[1] Lecky's "History of England," vol. 2, p. 216.
[2] Froude's "English in Ireland," Book V., c. 2, sect. 6.

price or die. The miserable tenant, having no other possible means of livelihood, accepted the former alternative, and the latter, too often, with it. The better class of tenant fled to America to escape the lawlessness of the law; the poverty-stricken remainder accepted injustice as the normal condition of life, and submitted to the exaction.

Such were the adverse circumstances in which the staple trade of Ireland had to be carried on during the greater part of the eighteenth century. We have now to consider the attitude of the legislature of Great Britain towards it. The fixed idea of the Parliament of Great Britain was that Ireland, like the colonies, existed solely for the benefit of the mother country. If the interests of Ireland or of the colonies came into competition with those of Great Britain, they must be crushed. If either Ireland or the colonies could be used for the advantage of Great Britain, they were but pawns in the game, to be protected or sacrificed as the exigencies of the case might require. This policy resulted not only in the loss of the American colonies, but also in a far greater loss—the permanent alienation of the Irish race.

The policy was carried out, in relation to Irish agricultural produce, in this fashion: that produce was prohibited, as a rule, from entry into Great Britain, and only a dribbling trade was conducted with France. But in times of war, when prices in Great Britain ruled high, or there was pressure in victualling the services, an embargo was suddenly laid upon Ireland's foreign trade, and the duties upon exports into Great Britain were temporarily suspended. When the need had passed away the embargo was removed, and the duties were re-imposed. The most flourishing trade could not continue to prosper when it was subjected to such irritating interference, far less the agricultural trade of Ireland, which was hampered by so many internal difficulties. The first necessity for healthy trade expansion is that it should be permitted to flow freely in such channels as it is able to cut out for itself. If its stream is suddenly interrupted and artificially forced in a new direction, it rarely, and only with great difficulty, resumes its original course. The trader who is forced at short notice to break contract finds it hard to regain his disappointed customer. He who is compelled to sell his goods in one market only is at the mercy of the purchaser in respect to prices. It is no marvel that, in the circumstances, Irish agriculture stagnated and that the Irish farmer failed to prosper.

It may, perhaps, be worth while to give an illustration of the manner in which the interests of Ireland were manipulated to promote those of England. Butter was one of the articles which

Ireland was, in the interests of the English farmer, prohibited from exporting to Great Britain. But the interests of British woollen trade required a plentiful supply of grease, and "stale and dirty butter, not fit for eating," served the purpose excellently. The British farmer naturally declined to allow his butter, for which he could find a plentiful market, to degenerate into this condition. So in 1763 an Act was passed, which, after reciting that spoilt butter was an essential ingredient in the manufacture of cloth, that there was a great scarcity of the commodity, and that the manufacture was thereby "greatly distressed," it was enacted that for five years grease butter might be imported from Ireland free of all rates, duties, penalties and forfeitures. And to make quite certain that sound butter was not surreptitiously imported under pretence of being grease butter, a special summary method of trying the case was established, and if the butter was found to be fit for food it was to be immediately confiscated.[1]

That Act epitomises the policy of Great Britain towards Ireland in relation to trade. If Ireland showed symptoms of developing an industry which might by chance compete with British enterprise or lower British profits, it was ruthlessly destroyed. If, on the other hand, her miseries could be turned to account for the

[1] 3 Geo. III., c. 20.

benefit of British trade, those miseries became valuable British assets. Ireland might not sell butter or cloth, but she might let her butter go rancid in order that Great Britain might manufacture cloth more cheaply. Great Britain sent to Ireland the stimulating message that one main agricultural product should be unavailable for commerce until it had become practically valueless.

Thus it came about that, at the time when England and Scotland were ready to take their great forward stride upon the road of commercial prosperity, in Ireland not only had prosperity been destroyed, but the very foundations upon which success might have been built up in the future had been obliterated. The commerce of Great Britain took its great leap forward after the Peace of Paris in 1763,[1] the year of the Irish Butter Bill. The war which was then terminated had been a trade war, and it resulted in the acquisition of sole markets for Great Britain in the whole of North America and in India. The woollen trade expanded rapidly; it was the age of rare developments in machinery and increased activity in iron foundries and potteries. But although Irishmen had fought by sea and land to achieve this result, it had not been for Ireland that they fought. The increased trade which followed the acquisition of new markets was not

---

[1] Thorold Rogers' "Industrial History," p. 15.

at all in agricultural produce; it was chiefly in textiles, and of these Ireland had none to offer except her coarse linens. When at last, in 1778-80, the Irish commercial restrictions were in part relaxed, trade had settled itself in a British groove, and would have remained there even if Ireland had possessed the capital and the energy to compete for it. But the only capital which she had hoarded was an accumulated reserve of wrongs, and the only energy which she possessed was expended in hatred of her oppressors. She had been beaten down to a lower plane of development and civilisation than that occupied by Great Britain, from which it was impossible for the trade relaxations or the Union to raise her — impossible, because they could not, from the nature of the case, place her upon an equality with England in respect to trade. Scotland had taken her independence to market and sold it for a valuable consideration; Ireland laid hers down in sullen and hopeless surrender. A century of repression had proved too hopeless a handicap in the race for prosperity. The acquiescence of Scotland in the Union dated from the time when she first felt the full benefit of commercial unity. Ireland, because she has been so grievously outdistanced, has never had any such reason for acquiescence.

But it may be urged that this argument carries us too far. If all chance of commercial prosperity for Ireland was in fact strangled by the policy of Great Britain during the eighteenth century, and if Scotch acquiescence in the Union was mainly due to her admission within the ring-fence of the protective policy of England—a boon which might have been conferred by federation—how is it possible that any concession to Ireland, whether of Home Rule or Federation, will produce the desired pacification? Neither policy will bestow upon her that trade prosperity which, it is contended, has been permanently lost. Such results cannot be achieved by tinkering the constitution. They are dependent upon circumstances which legislation may possibly foster, but which no law can create.

The facts have not been stated for the purpose of founding an argument that local self-government will restore prosperity to Ireland, although it might conduce to that result. They have been set forth to show that for historical reasons Ireland has been forced down to a lower, or at any rate a different, plane of development to that of England and Scotland, and that therefore unity of legislation and administration has been practically impossible. The necessity for separate legislation and administration has been one of the main causes of that paralysis of Parliament which has been shown to exist.

But it must be remembered that any special treatment of Ireland has not been advocated in the foregoing pages. The whole drift of the argument has been that our present system of government is prejudicial to the interests of each of the three countries forming the United Kingdom. It has been treated as a national, not as an Irish question—a question which England and Scotland are both interested in solving. If this be clearly perceived, it will be seen at once that even if the contention that local self-government could by no means restore, or even facilitate the restoration of commercial prosperity of Ireland were justifiable, it would not affect the question at issue. A national advantage must not be foregone because it fails to herald the millennium in one particular State.

CHAPTER XII

THE BURDEN OF IRELAND (*continued*)

EMPHASIS has been laid upon the trade relations of the three countries during the eighteenth century because they contain the solution of the problem which we have to investigate. There were, no doubt, other differences between the condition of Scotland and that of Ireland which nurtured content in the former and despair in the latter, not only in that century, but far on into its successor. The religion of the majority was established in Scotland, in Ireland it was persecuted. Scotch education was fostered and encouraged in accordance with the national wish, and in consequence flourished exceedingly; Irish education was made a weapon for Protestant proselytism, and the failure of the Charter schools is a matter of notoriety. The hedge school of the ostracised Catholic was a greater educational force than the endowed institutions of the dominant minority. Again, the "new agriculture" was introduced into Scotland by Scotch landlords, largely at their own expense. They were not altogether unselfish in their action. They knew that improved tillage meant enhanced rents, but in the result the tenant as well as the landowner profited from the reform. The new agriculture was never introduced into Ireland during the eighteenth century. The Irish landlord did nothing for the improvement of his estates. The "earth-hunger" enabled him to raise his rents without any such unnecessary expense. But all these differences are subsidiary to the main difference in commercial prosperity. Had Irish agriculture been allowed to develop unhampered by legislative restrictions, the landowner would, in all probability, have been induced, out of mere self-interest, if for no other consideration, to adopt a more generous policy towards the land tiller. Community of prosperity is the great solvent of religious differences. If the Catholic majority and the Protestant minority had been allowed to share with Great Britain the advantages which accrued from equality of trade, no religious enthusiasm would have been strong enough to drive either party into overt rebellion or secret conspiracy The restrictive laws are the keys of the situation.

Since the late Professor Seeley used the weight of his authority to justify the sanity of speculation upon what might have been the course of history "if some one event had fallen out differently,"[1] no one has dared to cast a stone at those who

[1] "The Expansion of England," p. 163.

have adopted this line of argument. Let us therefore consider for a moment what might have been the results if the Irish offer of union with England in 1704 had been accepted upon terms similar to those which were granted to Scotland, and that the union with Scotland had fallen through at some stage of its precarious negotiations. Ireland would then have been admitted to equality of trade with Great Britain. Her woollen manufacture, which had been strangled only five years before, would have revived. Possessing the finest grazing land, and producing the most excellent wool in the world, instead of smuggling the latter to France in exchange for claret and brandy, she would have manufactured it herself, and would have competed with England in the home, colonial and foreign markets. Her hemp and flax manufactures would never have been hampered, and under such favouring circumstances would have developed with rapidity. Her agricultural produce would have found a free market in its natural destination. She would have obtained the benefit of the Navigation Acts; and ships, Irish built and Irish manned, would have carried her products to all parts of the world. Her position would have given her unique facilities for prosecuting the colonial trade in textiles, and her southern harbours, Cork, for instance, would have had equal advantages with any English port for carrying on the Indian trade. If the reader will cast a glance at the map, he will see that Cork, Limerick, Galway and Sligo would have possessed immense advantages over Bristol, the port of the earlier part of the century, and over Liverpool, the port of the latter part, in competition for the colonial and West Indian trade. They would have had not less advantage over Glasgow, the creation of the British Customs Union. Is it not conceivable that, under such conditions, before the century had expired, Ireland would have attained to the prosperity and content which proved such a blessing to Scotland? Is it not conceivable also that the old hatred of England would have died out, and that Ireland, while retaining, as the Scotch retain, a distinct national sentiment, an undying love for the national literature, art, history and traditions, would have looked to England as a brother and a benefactor, not as an enemy and a tyrant?

And if Scotland had not obtained the benefits which flowed from commercial equality, is it not probable that she would have remained a thorn in the side of England? She would have had no colonial trade, and she would have been deprived of the benefit of the Navigation Acts. Her goods would have been excluded from England and England's colonies, and her commercial relations with foreign States would have been precarious. She would have remained a struggling agricultural community, with a trade of slight vitality, a low civilisation and an indelible hatred of the nation which prevented her commercial expansion.

Lest anyone should think that imagination has exaggerated the possibilities of the case, let us consider a short descriptive passage from the pen of an eighteenth century traveller.

"The common people are such in outward appearance as you would not at first take to be of the human species, and in their lives they differ but little from brutes, except in their love to spirituous liquors. They are extremely indigent, but had rather sustain poverty than labour. They have an implacable spirit of revenge, of which several instances happened during my stay there, but I know not whether that should be mentioned to their dishonour, since, in general, the same disposition which prompts a man to revenge an injury restrains him from doing one.

"The nastiness of the lower people is really greater than can be reported; under the same roof, and often with but one door to all, are the stable, cow-house and dwelling-place, without window or chimney; if they have the latter, it is generally covered to keep in the smoak, the warmth of which is very pleasant to them. And I could not but imagine that their way of living has a real effect upon their countenances, for the children I observed have good complections and regular features, but the faces of the men and women are coloured like smoak; their mouths wide, and their eyes sunk exactly as one pulls one's face when in the midst of a cloud of smoak. They wear their hair so long that it almost hides their faces, and covers a great part of their bodies. They use no shoes and stockings but on Sundays, and then they carry them in their hands to the entrance to the churchyard, and pull them off again as soon as service is over. The petticoats of the women seldom reach so low as their knees: they marry young, and are very prolific, so that in England, what would be thought an immense, is there reckoned but a moderate family. But their rudeness is beginning to go off, and they are already pretty well civilised in the trading towns where the knowledge of the use of money has made them eager enough to acquire it. Their progress in husbandry I mentioned before, and one town I visited, as I told your ladyship, is in a fair way of trade. Another little town is receiving £200,000 a year for linnen, and at a third they have set up manufactures with surprising success."[1]

Is it not a curiously accurate description of Irish life and manners; and is it not marvellous that after the lapse of 130 years the portrait should still appear so life-like? We can almost trace the course of the writer's journey. He

[1] "Gentleman's Magazine" (May, 1766), vol. 36, p. 209.

evidently started from Dublin, and after passing through the agricultural districts of Leinster, he entered Ulster; visited some of the smaller towns, and ended his pilgrimage, in all probability, at Belfast. He depicts scenes which every traveller in Ireland has witnessed — the smoky hovel in которой man and beast herd together; the angel-faced children, and the worn, grimed, prematurely-aged elders; the listlessness of the people who "had rather sustain poverty than labour." He notes also characteristics which are at any rate Irish by inveterate tradition: their improvident early marriages, and their huge families; their tendency to whiskey-drinking, their fiery temper prompting to frequent scuffles, yet moderated withal by generosity and kindliness. The description is Irish to the very letter.

Irish to the very letter indeed, but nevertheless it is not a description of Ireland. The writer is relating the observations which he made during a tour through the Lowlands of Scotland, through the heart of the district which is now throbbing with agricultural, industrial and commercial activity. The route was, apparently, from Carlisle to Dumfries, Ayr, Saltcoats, Paisley, Kilmarnock, Glasgow and Edinburgh. The three towns mentioned in the latter part of the quotation are Dumfries, Paisley and Kilmarnock. I have slightly garbled the text in order to remove the tell-tale names. The picture shows us the now cleanly, canny, provident, energetic Scot as he was in 1766—just at the period when equality of trade was beginning to tell for the benefit of his country, but before it had been long enough in operation to raise him permanently in the scale of civilisation. We peep through the curtain which the force of modern opinion has drawn over the past, and we find our Scotsman indistinguishable from " the mere Irish," and resembling his present descendants in no respect whatever.

Especial stress has been laid on these facts for two reasons. First, because they accentuate the proposition which has already been laid down, namely, that it was not the incorporating union which bestowed prosperity upon Scotland, but the equality of trade, which might have been secured by federation. The incorporating union had been in operation for sixty years when the above description was written. A generation had passed away, and yet the Lowland Scot remained an Irishman in his character and in his surroundings. From that date the effects of the policy of equality of trade began to tell, and the Scotsman was rapidly converted into a prudent, self-reliant, energetic being who has hardly his equal for those virtues in the whole world. The same transformation might easily have taken place in Ireland had the remedy of equality of trade been applied before it was too late; before Scotland and England had gained too long a start in the race for prosperity. But the trade relaxations of 1778-82 came too late. The seed of Irish prosperity was planted under the shade of the sturdy growths of England and Scotland. There was a slight revival of trade after 1782, but the ground in which it should have developed was already fully occupied and its growth was weakly. The incorporating union, when it was effected, had no virtue to heal the wounds of Ireland: she was permanently disabled. There is no reason therefore why we should expect to find Ireland passing through any period of acquiescence in that policy.

The other reason for which stress has been laid on the Scotch transformation of character is that, in passing to the second branch of our subject, the inquiry whether there are any reasons why the local self-government which Scotland demands should not be also conceded to Ireland, we are met on the threshold by what I will term the racial objection. It has been stated in various terms; notably, in one conspicuous instance, by an allusion to the Hottentots. More directly, and less offensively, the argument may be summed up as follows: The Irish are a Celtic race, and the Celtic races are notoriously unfitted for that form of constitutional government which is suited to races of Teutonic origin. Dislike for labour, disrespect for law, passionate assertion of individuality to the prejudice of the community, are bred in their bone and run in their blood. Like the higher order of animals, they are only serviceable and truly happy when they are rigidly controlled by whip, goad or rein. Self-government for them is synonymous with anarchy. According to Mr. Froude's formula—if I adopted his own terms in dealing with an opponent, I should say his " cant "—the Irish can only be prosperous under the rule of a benevolent autocrat.

The description which I have quoted of the condition of Scotland in the middle of the last century goes far to disprove the theory that national characteristics are permanent and ineradicable. In no one particular does that description tally with the Lowlanders of the present day. Anyone reading it thirty years after it was written would probably have denied its accuracy. So rapidly did changed conditions alter traits of character which were apparently national and permanent. Mr. Lecky has sufficiently exposed the hollowness of the contention.[1] By copious examples he has proved that those national characteristics which we are prone to consider permanent are more frequently ephemeral. They are the result of environment. A persistence of the same environment may tend to perpetuate them by the law of heredity, but on the other hand, a change of environment certainly tends to extirpate them. If the Irish

[1] " History of England," vol. 2, p. 381.

are conspicuous for disrespect for law, it is because they have been compelled for a long period to live under laws which they could not respect. When the vast majority of a people have been subjected to so draconian a code as the penal laws, which desecrated marriage, bribed the son to revolt against his father, outraged the elementary rights of property, and shut the door of every honourable profession, they would have been slaves indeed had they submitted with "respect." When every avenue of success for honest labour was closed by edicts which prevented agricultural and commercial enterprise, it was not wonderful that they should become listless and apathetic, and show themselves averse from work. Hemmed in thus on all sides by such cruel prohibitions, it is not surprising that at times, in a wild passion of despair, they avenged themselves with pike, pistol and dagger. The Irish were what their environment made them, and the maker of that environment was England.

And, although these conditions were greatly ameliorated at the end of the last century, Ireland has never been made to feel that, since the Union, she has been governed upon any other than the old theory that she is an appanage of England. The interests of Scotland may have been neglected by the British Parliament, but, since 1750, legislation has rarely or never been thrust upon the Scotch which was in principle a flagrant defiance of their deliberate opinion. But the mere suggestion that Ireland should be governed by "Irish ideas" is supposed to be stamped upon the face of it with absurdity. The accepted doctrine has been that Irish opinion ought not to count in the settlement of Irish questions.[1] When England is seized with a desire to render "Justice to Ireland," that justice is rendered according to "English ideas," and in defiance of the protests and warnings of Ireland's representatives. The English ideas may have been right, the Irish protest may have been absurd; that is not the question. In such circumstances it was impossible that any acquiescence in the policy of an incorporating union could be generated.

In considering the "racial argument," I have passed over the fact that the statement that the Irish are purely or mainly of Celtic origin is untrue, because, even on the assumption of its correctness, the reply is complete. It was the opinion of the late Professor Huxley that Ireland was, on the whole, more Teutonic in blood than the western portion of England. No one can read the story of the frequent invasions and plantations of Ireland from England and Scot-

---

[1] "No instance has been cited, and no instance could be cited, in which the House of Lords had resisted the will of the people when it was clearly ascertained. *I do not say that the House of Lords would attend to the opinion of Ireland itself.*"—Lord Salisbury at Bradford; *Times*, May 23rd, 1893.

land without coming to the conclusion that such a theory is probable. Mr. Froude, when he tells the story of those proceedings, has to admit that it was not long before the adventurers and colonists abandoned the habits and modes of thought of their ancestors and assumed those of the natives of the island. The fact is in itself proof that the supposed racial aptitudes and disabilities are merely skin deep, and are rapidly changed by change of environment. Mr. Froude, to account for it, instead of facing the facts, imagines a mysterious Irish mephitic atmosphere, or a species of *diabolus ex machinâ* which brought about the change: the antithesis of the Providence which he is so fond of marshalling on the side of his own argument. The theory lends itself to splendid invective, but it has little relation to reality. The anonymous observer of 1702, quoted by Mr. Lecky, laid bare the real cause of this strange phenomenon. "If," he wrote, "we had a new sette (of officers) taken out of London that had noe knowledge or engagements in Ireland, *yet in seven years they would carry a grudge in their hearts against the oppressions of England*, and as their interest in Irish ground increased, so would their aversion to the place they left. So it hath been these five hundred years; so it is with many of my acquaintance but lately come from England; and so it is likely to be till the interests be made one."[1]

[1] "History of England," vol. 2, p. 383.

But, it may be said, "However interesting and conclusive your argument may be, does it not end in upsetting your own case? You contend that Irish restlessness, resistance to order and want of perseverance are the result of centuries of misgovernment; that long continuance of adverse environment has stamped them deeper and deeper into the Irish character, and that heredity has assisted in perpetuating them. Granting these assertions, do they not prove that the Irish are at the present moment unfitted to manage their own affairs? We cannot go back upon history and undo the evil we have wrought; should we not be aggravating that evil by conferring the power of self-government upon a race which we have incapacitated for a judicious exercise of it?"

The amount of truth which lies in this contention represents the Nemesis which dogs the steps of misgovernment. Translated into terms of the constitution, it means that we have forced the will of the Irish minority upon the Irish majority for so long that it has at last become our duty to continue to do so. Evil, persisted in, becomes a necessity and is at last esteemed a virtue. It is more than probable that local self-government, when it is granted to Ireland, will work badly at first, for the very reason that the Irish are unversed in the art. We have not even allowed them the training of free municipal government, which has been so potent a factor in educating the administrative faculty in England and Scotland. Besides, many sinister influences will be at work to secure the failure of the experiment. Let us not delude ourselves with vain hopes, but rely rather upon the proved transience of national characteristics. We have seen in how short a time the Scotch character underwent transformation. There is nothing to prevent a similar transformation taking place in Ireland. The Irish, when they are removed from the depressing environment of their own country, become foremost in administrative business. We discover among them excellent generals, governors of colonies, civil servants, men of affairs. The talent for government is latent, waiting to be roused into activity. The contention that Ireland is unfit for the control of her local affairs has sufficient force in it to persuade us to proceed slowly with the process of devolution, in order that the aptitudes which are essential for the orderly conduct of government may have time to develop. It may urge us to move by steps rather than by leaps, but it has no sufficient force to induce us to abandon a policy which is necessary for the well-being, not only of the other two kingdoms, but also of the Empire.

CHAPTER XIII

THE BURDEN OF IRELAND (*continued*)

It is possible that another argument may be urged by those who are only partially convinced. "Why do you trouble yourself," they may say, "with hypothesis and speculation, when the question has been brought to the touchstone of experience? The experiment has been tried: the Irish have been entrusted with self-government. It may be admitted perhaps that, so long as Poynings' Act was in force; so long as no Irish law could be passed without the assent of the British Privy Council, the apparent self-government of Ireland was a mockery and a delusion; but surely from 1782 until the date of the Union, Ireland enjoyed a free constitution and virtual independence, so far as her own affairs were concerned. Yet the experiment ended in anarchy, which rendered the Union inevitable. A grain of experience is worth a pound of theory."

This argument, which is very freely used, is based upon a misconception of the facts of the case. Ireland has never enjoyed self-government in any intelligible sense of the term, and we are absolutely without precedent to show us how the Irish would conduct themselves if it were conferred upon them. It is necessary, for the sake of clearness, to anticipate a subsequent stage of our investigation, and to attempt a short definition of State rights in a federal constitution. State rights are the rights of legislation upon and administration of such matters as affect the interests of the members of the State, and no other interests whatsoever, in accordance with the wish of the majority of the legally elected representatives of that State, in Parliament assembled.

In order to test the extent to which the Irish constitution of 1782 corresponded with the terms of this definition, it is necessary briefly to consider the conditions of government prior to that date.

In respect to legislation, the Irish Parliament was controlled nominally by the Irish Act known as Poynings' Law,[1] but in reality by a later Irish Act, which interpreted the earlier statute.[2] The object of Poynings' Law is sufficiently indicated by its title: "An Act that no Parliament be holden in this land until the Acts be certified into England." The proposed legislation had to be prepared by the English Government in Ireland, and submitted to the English Privy

---

[1] Irish Statutes. 10 Hen. VII., c. 4 (1495).
[2] *Ib.*, 3 and 4 P. and M., c. 11 (1556).

Council. If it was approved, an Irish Parliament could be summoned to accept or reject it. Such a system of legislation was manifestly unworkable. If Parliament was to be allowed to retain even the semblance of authority, it was necessary that it should be something more than a registering assembly with a right of veto. An explanatory Act was therefore passed in 1556, which gave the Irish Parliament the power of initiation. That Parliament was permitted to pass "heads" of bills. These were transmitted by the Irish Privy Council to the English Privy Council. The latter could either approve, amend or reject those bills. In the two former cases, the bills were returned to Ireland, and the Irish Parliament could either accept them, with such amendments, if any, as had been introduced in England, or they could reject them, but no further amendment was possible.

The only real advantage which was effected by this amendment of Poynings' law was that it was possible for the opinion of the Irish Parliament to find expression upon matters of legislation. But it must be evident that Parliament had no power to effect legislation. The supreme legislature for Ireland was, in reality, the English Privy Council. Ireland was, in fact, a dependent State, to which the dominant State conceded the semblance of local self-government.

In regard to administration, the sham was

even more apparent. Ministers were appointed by England, and they were in no way responsible to the Irish Parliament. Parliament was reduced to the impotence of a debating society: it was merely the arena for a display of brilliant but sterile dialectics.

Members were therefore affixed with no responsibility for their actions, because no parliamentary consequences followed upon either their words or their votes. It is not of much importance how such a House of Commons was constituted, but it should be borne in mind that the vast majority of the people were unrepresented in it. The Catholics on the one hand, and the Dissenters on the other, were excluded from the franchise. The borough representation, moreover, was as much in the hands of the great landowners as were the English and Scotch boroughs at the same period. One result only could follow from such a system of government. In Great Britain the recklessness of opposition was restrained by the knowledge that in certain contingencies the party might be called upon to take up the reins of government. In Ireland no such check prevailed. The minority knew that they were powerless to influence the course of events by legitimate parliamentary action, but they knew also that outside the House there was a vast army of malcontents ready to applaud the most reckless violence of speech. The only road to fame was by appeal to the passions of the mob, and the Irish politician was powerful in proportion to his eloquence. Government, on the other hand, had no fear of a constitutional opposition to restrain it from ruling Ireland in the interests of England and of the episcopal minority. Its only dread was lest a patriot leader should, by force of eloquence and invective, excite the passions of the populace to a too dangerous degree. When that condition arose they endeavoured to silence him by bribery. The Irish establishment was overloaded with sinecure places and with pensions. When a patriot became a source of embarrassment, a sinecure office was found for him. In a poverty-stricken country like Ireland, where the avenues to wealth and fame were few, and where political ambition could never receive its legitimate reward in political responsibility, such malpractices were bound to meet with too much success. The opposition members showed the strange combination of brilliant rhetoric and keen-nosed place-hunting. Such was the training in constitutional government which England inflicted on Ireland.

It must be observed that the English and British Parliaments had always asserted, and had frequently exercised, the right of legislating upon Irish State affairs. In 1720 the British Parliament availed itself of the opportunity afforded by an attempt on the part of the

Irish House of Lords to exercise the functions of an Irish Court of Final Appeal, to pass a declaratory statute,[1] which not only denied the right of the Irish House of Lords to exercise any jurisdiction whatever, but also asserted the right of the British Parliament "to bind the kingdom and people of Ireland by statute." It is worth noting, however, that this right was exercised far more frequently before the passing of this Act than after it. The great subject upon which England then legislated for Ireland was the title to land, which had been rendered so uncertain by the various confiscations and restorations of the seventeenth century. But these questions were practically settled before the end of Queen Anne's reign.

It is necessary to refer to this statute because, without so doing, it would be impossible to understand the nature of the so-called "constitution" of 1782. The methods by which that constitution was created were these. On May 16th, 1782, the following resolutions were moved and carried without a dissentient voice in the British Parliament: (1) "That it is the opinion of this Committee that an Act, made in the 6th year of the reign of his late Majesty King George I., intituled 'An Act for the better securing the dependency of the Kingdom of Ireland upon the Crown of Great Britain,' ought to be repealed."

---

[1] 6 Geo. I., c. 5.

(2) "That it is the opinion of this Committee that it is indispensable to the interests and happiness of both kingdoms that the connection between them should be established, by mutual consent, upon a permanent and solid basis."[1] These resolutions were reported to the House and agreed to. Leave was given to bring in a bill for the repeal of the statute 6 Geo. I., c. 5, and the second resolution was adopted in the form of an address to the Crown. The two resolutions were on the following day carried in the House of Lords, and in the same session 6 Geo. I., c. 5, was repealed.[2]

Such was the action of the British Government so far as legislation was concerned. They contemplated that the exact relations of the federal constitution between England and Ireland would be regulated "upon a permanent and solid basis" by treaty; that "a negotiation would be entered into with commissioners authorised by the Irish Parliament to determine finally and definitely the exact limits of the independence, the superintending power of England in matters of trade, the consideration to be given by Ireland for protection, and the share to be contributed by her for the general support of the Empire."[3] Manifestly these

---

[1] Parl. Hist., vol. 23, c. 28.
[2] 22 Geo. III., c. 53.
[3] Lecky's "History of England," vol. 4, p. 550.

negotiations should have preceded the legislative action of the British Parliament. The settlement of the points in question was vital to the establishment of a permanent federal government. The perversity of Grattan and the irritated sensitiveness of the Irish stood in the way of such a consummation. Grattan urged that the claim of Ireland must be conceded as a matter of right and could not be made a question of barter. There is no ground for doubting that Grattan honestly and loyally desired State self-government for Ireland subject to a federal union with Great Britain. He failed to perceive that, in refusing to define the terms of the federal union, he was reducing the relations between England and Ireland to the alternative of separation or absolute incorporation.

Poynings' law and its amending Act, being statutes of the Irish Parliament, were left to that assembly to deal with. They were not expressly repealed, but an Act was passed which regulated the methods of legislation for the future.[1] It provided that the Irish Privy Council must certify to the Crown all such Acts as might be passed by the Irish Parliament, and none other, without addition, diminution or alteration, and that they should become law if they were returned to Ireland under the Great Seal of Great Britain,

[1] Irish Statutes, 21 and 22 Geo. III., c. 47.

without alteration, diminution or addition, and not otherwise.

These two sets of operations on the part of the British and Irish Parliaments were intended to constitute the basis of the new relations between the two countries in the absence of any definite treaty, which seemed to be unattainable. But almost immediately a question of legal casuistry was raised in the Irish Parliament. The English Parliament had, it was said, exercised the right of legislating for Ireland before the declaratory Act of 1720. The mere repeal of that Act could not be construed as an abolition of the constitutional right, and England might in the future reassert it. Consequently, in 1783, the Parliament of Great Britain passed an Act of renunciation, whereby it was declared that the right claimed by the people of Ireland "to be bound only by laws enacted by his Majesty and the Parliament of that kingdom in *all cases whatever*, and to have all actions and suits at law or in equity, which may be instituted in that kingdom, decided by his Majesty's courts therein finally, and without appeal from thence . . . . shall be, and it is hereby declared to be, established and ascertained for ever, and shall at no time hereafter be questioned or questionable."[1]

It must be observed, in the first place, that the terms of this declaration go far beyond any

[1] 23 Geo. III., c. 28.

conceivable definition of a federal union. The modern idea of a federated State is that it should have absolute control only of such matters as affect the rights and interests of that State, and none other. The declaratory statute of the British Parliament released Ireland from the obligation to render obedience to any law that had not been passed by the Irish Parliament. It left Ireland free to legislate separately for national defence and the expense of the war establishment, and in regard to foreign relations. It even left the question of succession to the throne doubtful. If circumstances had arisen which compelled Great Britain to pass another Act of Settlement, that Act would not have bound the people of Ireland. The relations were not federal, they were those of two confederated States bound together by the imperfect tie of a common sovereign.

In a very short time these defects made themselves apparent in practice. The question of the succession to the crown came indirectly into question in the struggle upon the Regency when George III. was incapacitated by madness in 1788. The British Government, for reasons which need not be stated here, decided to constitute the Regent by Act of Parliament, and not by address.[1] But that Act of Parliament when passed would not have constituted

[1] Lecky: "History of England," vol. v., p. 106.

the Regent for Great Britain the Regent for Ireland also, because it would not have bound Ireland. The only tie between the two countries was temporarily dissolved. The Irish Parliament resolved to make the Prince of Wales Regent of Ireland by an address from both Houses. If that address had been presented at once the Prince of Wales would have been Regent of Ireland and not Regent of England. He would have exercised unlimited regal power within Ireland, with the important exception that he could not have assented to a single Irish bill because he would not have controlled the British Great Seal, which alone could convert an Irish bill into an Irish Act. But the Lord Lieutenant refused to transmit the address to England. The Irish Parliament appointed commissioners to perform the task. They presented it indeed, but only at the moment when the King had recovered his reason, and the question of a Regency was at an end.[1]

This is merely a specimen of the manifold difficulties which arose from the incoherence of the constitutional arrangement of 1782-3. Similar difficulties manifested themselves in other directions, in the questions of the commercial arrangements between the two countries, and of the amount which Ireland should contribute towards the national defence. It is clear that Ireland

---
[1] Froude: "English in Ireland," Book VII., chap. 2, sect. 5.

might, constitutionally, have imposed prohibitive tariffs upon British goods, and have declined to raise a soldier or man a ship in time of war. The attention of the Irish Parliament, which should have been concentrated upon the regeneration of Ireland, was dissipated over a series of questions which ought to have been settled before legislative freedom was accorded to it.

It must be evident, therefore, that on the legislative side the constitution of 1782 was so faulty that it could not contain within itself the germ of permanence. It was upon the administrative side, however, that its defects were most glaring. Although legislative independence was practically conceded to Ireland, the other arm of local self-government, administrative independence, was denied her. Ireland was free to enact her own laws, but she was powerless to control the administration of those laws. An adverse vote in the Irish House of Commons produced no effect whatever upon the Government. The administration was appointed by the British Cabinet. The fall of a British Cabinet in London produced a change of government in Ireland, even though the outgoing Irish administration might possess the confidence of the Irish House of Commons, and the incoming administration might be distrusted and disliked. The Irish politician remained powerless to control the destinies of his country, and could only hope to influence Government by appeals to the passions of the disfranchised majority of the people. After fourteen years' unavailing effort to evolve order from such chaos, the constitutional leaders of the Irish party retired from Parliament, leaving the conduct of the tragic sequel to the demagogue and the conspirator.

Such a system was necessarily doomed to failure. It was a parody of and an insult to the idea of self-government. It taught the Irish, in terms which no man could fail to understand, that the most apparently liberal concessions that Great Britain could grant were but as the apples of the Dead Sea. Self-government was rendered a farce and a fraud solely on account of the influence which the English Government exerted over the Irish administration. The only discernible road of escape from that influence was by complete independence. For that independence Ireland fought; her struggle failed, and the incorporating union was the result.

In such circumstances it is impossible to contend that the union was the result of "a common national feeling" or "a sense of common interests,"[1] the sentiments which are presumed to impel nations to an incorporating union. Neither country was conscious of any common interest or feeling whatever, and, what

[1] Dicey: "Law of the Constitution," p. 132.

was worse for the eventual success of the union, neither of them received a compensating advantage from the transaction. In the case of England and Scotland, England obtained a guarantee of national security, and Scotland obtained increased facilities for trade expansion. There was no such mutuality of benefit in the union between Great Britain and Ireland. The union was, like the union with Scotland, in effect, a conquest, but unlike the union with Scotland, it was not a peaceful conquest. It was the outcome of a barbarous rebellion barbarously repressed. It satisfied no need, whether transient or permanent, of which the absorbed nation was conscious, and it did not, therefore, contain within itself the salve which could heal the wounds of a people smarting under a sense of a grievous national injury.

The results of this investigation from the historical standpoint are :—

1. That each of the three countries included in the incorporating union are conscious, to a greater or less degree, of disadvantages that arise from that union.

2. That in England this consciousness is intermittent. It is found in activity only at those times when the composition of the House of Commons is such that the will of the majority of Englishmen is overruled by the will of the minority.

3. That the relations with Scotland are, and always have been, of a character which demand a federal rather than an incorporating union; that considerations of a purely transient nature prevented the operation of the normal forces which make for federation; that Scotland ultimately acquiesced in the incorporating union chiefly on account of benefits which might with equal ease have been conferred upon her by federation; and that latterly, and precisely at the date when the paralysis of Parliament commenced, Scotland awoke to a sense of her need for separate administration and legislation, which has been partially and imperfectly gratified.

4. That in Ireland the conditions which made for union were always less apparent than in the case of Scotland; that the trade policy of England during the sixteenth and seventeenth centuries had so destroyed the possibility of commercial prosperity for Ireland that she was forced down to a lower level of civilisation than that of the sister kingdoms, from which she has never recovered; that the union, when it was effected, offered no advantage to Ireland which compensated for the surrender of nationality, and it did not, therefore, contain within itself the solvent of the national sentiment. These conclusions are merely an expansion of propositions 5 and 6.[1]

[1] See *ante*, p. 20.

Before passing to consider the nature of and objections to federal government and the possibility of adapting our present constitution to a federal system, it will be well to recapitulate once more the conclusions which have already been reached. We have found:—

1. That Parliament, through over-pressure of business, has been, since about 1850, incapable of transacting efficiently all the legislative and administrative business which is demanded of it.

2. That this over-pressure has resulted from the increasing demands for separate legislation and administration by England, Scotland and Ireland, and more especially from the separate demands of England.

3. That these separate demands still tend to increase, to the injury, not only of the interests of each State, but of Imperial interests.

4. That the injury to Imperial interests affects more especially those which relate to foreign and colonial affairs.

5. That the working of the present system is sapping the fundamental doctrine of all constitutional and democratic government, namely, that all laws shall be assented to by the majority of the representatives of those who will be compelled to obey them.

6. That it tends to divest members of Parliament of responsibility to their constituents.

7. That it tends to encourage the formation of small political groups in Parliament.

8. That each nation is to a greater or less degree conscious of these disadvantages, or of some of them, and is seeking, with more or less definiteness of aim, to escape from them.

9. That the causes which brought about the incorporating unions did not originate in the permanent desires or needs of the incorporated States.

CHAPTER XIV

THE LIFTING OF THE BURDENS

Having thus established a series of propositions, each of which reveals a weakness in our present constitution, and taken together, form a serious impeachment of its efficiency to meet the present needs of the nation, it is now necessary to consider whether any remedy is possible or practicable, and whether such remedy would entail fresh evils which would neutralise the advantages gained from it.

The arguments contained in the foregoing chapters have all converged towards one point, namely, to show that the necessary remedy is the adoption of some form of federal government in the place of the present unitarian system. Those arguments have been ill stated if the reader is prepared to deny the allegation that our system of government is an endeavour to govern a federation of States under the guise of unity, and that all its faults are due to the attempt to ignore this fundamental and immutable fact. Lest such a denial should be forthcoming, it will be shown, when the nature of a federal constitution is more rigidly defined, that it offers a remedy for each of the evils which have been enumerated.

But first it is necessary to examine the conditions which are held to be essential to any form of federal constitution. " There must exist," says the ablest exponent of the subject, " in the first place, a body of countries . . . so closely connected by locality, by history, by race, or the like, as to be capable of bearing in the eyes of their inhabitants an impress of common nationality. It will also be generally found . . . that lands which now form part of a federal State were at some stage of their existence bound together by close alliance or by subjection to a common sovereign. It would be going further than facts warrant to assert that this earlier connection is essential to the formation of a federal State, but it is certain that where federalism flourishes it is in general the slowly-matured fruit of some earlier and looser connection.

"A second condition, absolutely essential to the founding of a federal system, is the existence of a very peculiar state of sentiment among the inhabitants of the countries which it is proposed to unite. They must desire union, but they must not desire unity. If there be no desire to unite there is clearly no basis for federalism. . . . If, on the other hand, there be a desire for unity, the wish will naturally find satisfaction, not under a federal, but under a unitarian constitution. . . . The phase of sentiment, in short, which forms a necessary condition for the formation of a federal State is that the people of the proposed State should wish to form for many purposes a single nation, yet should not wish to surrender the individual existence of each man's State. We may perhaps go a little farther, and say that a federal government will hardly be formed unless many of the inhabitants of the separate States feel a stronger allegiance to their own State than to the federal State represented by the common government. . . . The sentiment therefore which creates a federal State is the prevalence throughout the citizens of more or less allied countries of two feelings which are to a certain extent inconsistent—the desire for national unity, and the determination to maintain the independence of each man's separate State. The aim of federalism is to give effect as far as possible to both these sentiments."[1]

We find, therefore, that four conditions may combine to generate a federal government. Two of them are essential, two will probably be found in existence.

The essential conditions are:—

1. The existence of a body of countries so

---

[1] Dicey: "Law of the Constitution," pp. 131-133. The omitted portions are illustrations.

closely connected by (*a*) locality, (*b*) history and (*c*) race as to be capable of bearing, in the eyes of their inhabitants, an impress of common nationality.

2. That the inhabitants of those countries must desire unity, and also, for certain purposes, to maintain the independence of each man's separate State.

The probable conditions are :—

1. That the federated States were at some period anterior to federation bound together by the looser tie of alliance or subjection to a common sovereign.

2. That the inhabitants of each State should feel stronger allegiance to their own State than to the federal State.

It can hardly be disputed that the essential conditions are, on the whole, fulfilled by the relations of the three States which compose the United Kingdom. That they are not sufficiently connected by locality, history and race to be capable of bearing an impress of common nationality need hardly be argued, since those conditions have been deemed strong enough to justify an incorporating union. That each of them desires unity and also State independence may perhaps be questioned. It may be asserted that England desires unity and not State independence : that Scotland desires unity, but stands doubtful upon the question of State rights, and that Ireland desires State independence but not unity.[1] If that were so, one of the forces which make for federation would be inoperative, but it would not necessarily follow that federation was on that account undesirable. Let us consider the three cases separately. It is alleged that England desires unity, and has no desire for State rights. It is hardly an accurate statement of England's attitude. She desires unity, no doubt; but it is not correct to say that she does not desire untrammelled control of those affairs which solely affect her interests. She is not constantly asserting the latter desire because, on account of her predominance in parliamentary representation, she usually maintains her control of them. But when, as during the Parliament of 1892-5, she loses that control she is lusty in her complaints. And such complaints can mean nothing but that she desires to maintain her State independence. She prefers doing so by methods which deprive the sister States of control over their own State affairs, but that does not alter the fact that she does, at bottom, desire to protect her separate rights. One of the most effective posters used in England at the General Election of 1895 bore the simple

---

[1] "Whether in the case of two countries, of which the one has no desire for State rights, and the other has no desire for union, the bases of a federal scheme are not wanting, is an inquiry which deserves consideration."—Dicey's "England's Case against Home Rule," p. 162.

question: "Why should England be governed by the Irish?" The answer is equally simple, namely, that in certain events the constitution provides that the English shall be so governed. But this was by no means the reply which the querist desired. His object was to induce the electors to return so large a body of members of his own way of thinking to Parliament that English State rights might be maintained even under a unitarian system of government, regardless of the fact that this was not a solution of the evil, but merely a shifting of the burden to Scotch and Irish shoulders. The placard is typical of the appeal which was made by one political party at the election of 1895, and the response of the electors proved, at any rate, that they were not apathetic in regard to the State interests of England. They doubtless desired to preserve the incorporating union, but they also desired to assert State rights. The conditions are those which make for federalism, but England has not yet perceived that the two aims are incompatible with justice to the other States.

Let us now turn to Scotland, whose opinion, it is alleged, is doubtful upon the subject. Having regard to the facts which have been brought out in our historical survey, there can be little hesitation in deciding which way the balance is inclined to turn. No one can have read the foregoing sketch of the history of the revulsion of Scotch feeling upon the subject of the Union without coming to the conclusion that Scotch opinion is slowly but surely travelling in the direction of the demand for State control of State affairs. At the same time the Scotch are earnest and sincere in their desire to maintain a federal unity. An expression of that desire forms the exordium of nearly every speech upon the question which has been delivered by Scotch members in Parliament. Scotland, it may therefore be concluded, is nearer than England to the typical condition which makes for federation.

In the case of Ireland, it is asserted, the conditions of England are reversed: that Ireland desires State rights, but she does not desire unity. It would be perhaps a little strange, in view of the history of Ireland's relations with Great Britain, if she expressed her desire for federal unity either frequently or with any great fervency. Her great need of State liberty is driven home to her consciousness with such force that it impairs the perception of the fact that federal unity is as essential to her existence as State independence, and sometimes, in moments of exasperation, responsible politicians have expressed themselves in terms which may be construed into an advocacy of separation. But the measured statements of Irish leaders, of Grattan and of O'Connell, of Butt and of Parnell, have always assumed and have often advocated the maintenance of a federal tie. It is sometimes alleged that this was due to deliberate deceit upon their part; that they were all separatists at heart, but that they did not dare to avow their secret opinions. The assertion is one which assumes an omniscience and a power to probe unexpressed motive to which I cannot pretend, and it must therefore be left to stand unanswered for what it is worth. In every country which has laboured long under the conviction that it is unjustly governed there will be found a residuum of restless persons who are prepared to proceed to extremities. It is not denied that there may be still some latent Fenianism in Ireland, but separation is not, at any rate, the policy which is usually publicly advocated on Irish platforms or in the Irish press. The Irish would doubtless be willing, if they could secure local self-government, to leave Imperial concerns alone. But that willingness is not necessarily due to a desire for separation; it is due to the overwhelming pressure of internal need, and to a conviction that Ireland is less interested in the solution of many Imperial problems than are the sister kingdoms.

We may perhaps summarise the respective attitudes of the three nations thus: England desires unity, but she has also a sub-consciousness of the necessity for maintaining State independence; Scotland desires unity, and also to a considerable degree, State independence; Ireland desires State independence, but she has also a sub-consciousness of the necessity for unity. These attitudes are by no means identical, but they nevertheless indicate the existence of those essential conditions which make for federation.

Of the two probable conditions, the first is most certainly fulfilled. At the period anterior to the time when federation might and probably would have been effected, had it not been for the intrusion of perturbing and adverse forces of a transient character, Scotland was bound to England by an alliance which resulted from the succession of a Scotch king to the throne of England. Ireland, before 1800, was in fact subject to the sovereignty of the English and British Parliament, although that subjection was, from 1782 to 1800, skilfully disguised. The question is not one of any great importance. It is merely a matter of interest to note how accurately all the conditions have been fulfilled which form the bases of federation in the opinion of the most learned and subtle opponent of the adoption of a federal system for the United Kingdom.

The existence of the second "probable" condition is more difficult to demonstrate. It would be idle to assert that inhabitants of England feel stronger allegiance to their own State than to the United Kingdom, because the preponderance of their influence blinds them, as a rule, to the distinction between the two. It would also be difficult to deny that Scotchmen, on the whole, feel a stronger allegiance to the United Kingdom than to Scotland. But there is nevertheless a definite latent sentiment of nationality in the Scottish people which is quite capable of developing into activity. The history of their opposition to so inconsiderable a matter as "The Small Notes Bill"[1] is sufficient to prove this. But the reverse sentiment is predominant in Ireland. The vast majority of Irishmen avow a stronger allegiance to Ireland than to the United Kingdom, and even the Irish supporters of the incorporating union are not altogether emancipated from a consciousness of that allegiance. The existence of this condition is the least demonstrable of the four which we have considered, but it must be noted that Professor Dicey does not put it forward as an essential condition, or even as one the existence of which can be very strongly presumed. It is one, moreover, which can merely be discussed hypothetically in regard to a case in which, although the essential conditions which make for federation are present, federal and States governments are non-existent.

Having thus ascertained that the bases upon

[1] See *ante*, p. 145.

which a federation may be founded are discernible beneath the form of our constitutional system, it is now necessary to consider two objections which, if they could be successfully maintained, would render the foregoing inquiry sterile of practical result.

It is objected: (1) That it is a "natural deduction from the general history of federalism" that "a confederation is an imperfect political union, transitory in its nature, and tending either to pass into one really united State or to break up into the different States which compose the federation";[1] and (2) that federation "is not, at any rate as it has hitherto been applied, a plan for disuniting the parts of a united State."[2]

The second objection is a corollary to the first. If it be true that the necessary tendency of government, in the case of all States which have certain common interests, is from separation, through federation to unity, it follows almost of necessity that when unity is achieved the process will not be reversed. If the "natural law" governing such cases is centripetal, it is unreasonable to expect that its effects should be centrifugal.

We here for the first time find the method of "comparative politics" applied to the solution of the problem. Now that method, although it

[1] Dicey's "England's Case against Home Rule," p. 192.
[2] *Ib.*, p. 161.

is of extreme interest and value in determining questions in relation to archaic communities, is by no means reliable when it is applied to modern politics. It may be useful, when the reform of some specific function of government is under discussion, to consider how the matter is ordered in other polities, but it is dangerous to draw large generalisations from a comparison of cognate systems, more especially when those generalisations deal with future as well as with present and past history. It might with some plausibility be maintained that constitutional government with a limited monarchy is an imperfect political organisation tending either to pass into republicanism or to relapse into the despotism from which it originated. But the assumption would be a dangerous, and at the same time a fruitless generalisation. It would help to solve no practical problem. All forms of government are the result of the special needs and environments of the governed. Unless it can be shown that the conditions of the cases to be compared are practically identical, the comparison is not only useless, but misleading. Let it be admitted for a moment that the tendency of Swiss federalism is towards a unitarian republic. The needs of a small nation surrounded on all sides by vast military States might well force development in that direction. But such an event would not raise the slightest presumption that the federal system of the United States, a country which is absolutely free from any such pressure, was tending in the direction of incorporating unity. And suppose again that in the future the United States, on account of the vastness of its territory and population, and the complexity of modern civilisation, should break up into a number of independent communities—say, eighteen unitarian republics, each roughly equivalent in area to the area of the French Republic—such a development would raise no presumption whatever that Switzerland would similarly break up into a series of independent States the size of the smaller English counties. The comparative method is useless where the basis of comparison is lacking.

Every federal government is based upon the special needs of the federated States, and until those needs change, or other requirements come into existence, it is unreasonable to suppose that the federal system will either merge into an incorporating union or will dissolve into separate and independent States. The Germanic Federation was called into being by the necessity of common resistance to a common foe, and its federal polity is based upon the necessity of placing under the federal government the control of all the means and facilities for resisting aggression. It is conceivable that, in the event of a foreign foe no longer threatening the interests of the States which make up the federation, they would return to their original independence; but is any development conceivable short of conquest by Prussia which will induce those States to surrender the control of their State affairs and empower the Reichstag to pass laws, on one day for Saxony, on another for Brunswick, and on a third for Hanover? The Austro-Hungarian Federation was the result of a long-continued intestine feud, originating in the dislike of Hungary to an incorporating union. Can it be contended that the remedy is in itself a stage in the journey towards a condition which was the original cause of difference?

It is true that certain early and amorphous federations, such as the connection between Denmark and Sweden, and between Spain and Portugal, to which reference has already been made,[1] have proved transitory, but such relations have generally been the consequence of some political exigency unconnected with the needs of the governed, or of conquest or threat of irresistible force. It may perhaps be laid down that where federation is the result of a voluntary surrender of certain powers for the collective benefit of the federating States, the constitution tends to prove stable, but where it is the result of causes which have no relation to the permanent needs of the federating States, it is apt to prove

[1] See *ante*, p. 134.

ephemeral. But this is true, not only of federations, but of all forms of government. If a unitarian system does not accord with the proved needs of the governed, it will possess no greater stability.

It may be concluded then that there is no such general law guiding the development and decay of federations as that which is laid down in the first objection which has been quoted. The corollary falls with it. It will be noted that the objection is largely conditional. Federation "is not, *at any rate as it has hitherto been applied*, a plan for disuniting the parts of a united State." The case of Austro-Hungary might be cited, were it worth while, in reply to this assertion, but the illustration would not help the present argument. The contention throughout has been that there is no evidence whatever in favour of the asserted general law in regard to the inception and decay of federal governments; that a government must be federal or unitarian in accordance with the needs of those who are governed. If it can be shown that the conditions of a unitarian State are in spirit and essence federal, the change from unity to federalism is progress, not relapse.

IV

THE NATURE OF FEDERATION

CHAPTER XV

THE OBJECTIONS TO FEDERATION

WE have now ascertained that the permanent conditions of the three States which have been incorporated into the United Kingdom are such as usually give rise to a federal and not to a unitarian constitution. We have also ascertained, in our historical retrospect, that the forces which ultimately determined events in favour of incorporating union were forces of transient political importance in no way relating to the permanent needs of the incorporated countries. We are now free to pass on to consider the nature of federal government, and the objections which can be urged against it, both in the abstract and in relation to its adoption by the United Kingdom.

A federal constitution is a constitution under which the affairs common to two or more States are conducted by a central legislature and executive, and the affairs peculiar to each federated State are conducted by a legislature and executive controlling those affairs and none other. Professor Dicey defines federalism happily in the following terms: " Whatever concerns the nation as a whole should be placed under the control of the national government. All matters which are not primarily of common interest should remain in the hands of the several States."[1]

A federal constitution is alleged to differ from a unitarian constitution, under which all functions of government including the power to alter the constitution itself are vested in one sovereign body, in the following essentials :—

1. That the constitution must be supreme; that is to say, it must not be within the competence of either the federal or of the States governments to vary any of its provisions.[2]

2. That each government, whether federal or State, is a non-sovereign law-making body, whose powers are limited and controlled by a law which it cannot alter.[3]

3. That since there is a law of the constitution controlling both federal and States governments, there must of necessity exist in the courts of justice a power to decide whether the Acts of the federal or of the States governments are valid within the terms of the constitution.

The first essential to federalism involves three further conditions :—

1. That the supreme constitution must be

---

[1] "The Law of the Constitution," p. 134.
[2] *Ib.*, p. 135.   [3] *Ib.*, p. 140.

either immutable, that is, that it cannot be changed by any procedure recognised by the constitution itself, or that it can only be changed by some legislative body, not the federal or the States government, summoned for that particular purpose.

2. That the supreme constitution must be a written constitution.

3. That the supreme constitution will be a "rigid" constitution; that is, it will be altered with far greater difficulty than is the case in a unitarian constitution.

These propositions are all based, to a great extent, upon the provisions of the constitution of the United States. It is a fact that they are also practically true in regard to the Swiss constitution, which is, in many respects, a mechanical copy of that of the United States. But forms of government, like all other human institutions, are, as we have already said, adjusted to the special needs of those who devise them, and must necessarily be considerably moulded by earlier constitutional evolutions. Let us consider for a moment how it came about that the United States constitution was a written constitution, and that the federal government was rendered powerless to modify it.

The colonies which, after the War of Independence, formed the basis of the United States had, previously to the Union, been subject to a common sovereign, namely, the Parliament of Great Britain. In this respect they fulfilled the first of the "probable conditions" which make for federation.[1] When they decided to reject that common sovereignty, they were in the condition of independent States, bound together by a temporary alliance for a specific purpose. There existed no body of law or custom which could be interpreted as a common constitution. If they desired to federate, they were compelled to adopt a written constitution.

A written constitution was therefore inevitable, but was it equally necessary that the supreme revising power should be entrusted to some body not the federal government? Why was not the federal government entrusted with the power of revision, and the rigidity which is attributed to all forms of federal government avoided? The answer is to be found in the relations of the uniting States. They had hitherto been bound together by no mutual bond save that of a common danger. They fulfilled the second "probable condition" which makes for federation. The inhabitants of each State felt a stronger allegiance to their own State than to the (contemplated) federal State. A strong sentiment of allegiance to the non-existent was hardly to be expected. The dominant desire of each State was to protect State rights against

---

[1] See *ante*, p. 227.

the possible inroads of a federal government, of whose workings none of the uniting States had any experience. And the device adopted to effect this was that of putting the power of constitutional revision outside the functions of the federal government.[1]

But, because these two constitutional results arose from the peculiar needs and conditions of the uniting States, it does not inevitably follow that they are necessary to all federal systems, although they may perhaps raise a presumption to that effect. Because a body of States desiring federation, but having no common constitutional law whatever, find it necessary to adopt a written constitution, it is no proof that another body of States desiring federation, but possessing an elaborate system of constitutional law and custom, must needs follow the same course. Nor, because such a body of States, having no experience whatever of a central system of government, decides to place the revision of the constitution beyond the control of that central government, does it follow that a similar body of States having long experience of the working of such a government might not come to an opposite conclusion. Seeing that all systems of federation are comparatively modern, these rapid generalisations from one or two cases are possibly rash.

[1] See Bryce, "American Commonwealth," chap. 3.

But it is contended that, if the central government possesses the power of constitutional revision, the arrangement is not a true federation. "If," says Professor Dicey, "Congress could legally change the constitution, New York and Massachusetts would have no legal guarantee for the amount of independence reserved to them under the constitution, and would be as subject to the sovereign power of Congress as is Scotland to the sovereignty of Parliament: the Union would cease to be a federal State, and would become a unitarian republic."[1]

The objection, as stated, involves a manifest confusion of thought. The contention is that, if the State of New York were liable to have its State rights restricted or abrogated by the central government, it would therefore be as little self-governing as Scotland, which has no State rights whatever. The statement that a congeries of States which can, through the action of a central government, abolish the federation is in fact a unitarian government, refutes itself. It confuses the possible with accomplished fact. Congress might possess the power to restrict or abrogate State rights, and yet, if the power were not exercised, the form of government would be as essentially federal as it is at the present moment. By no straining of terms could it be properly defined as a unitarian republic.

---

[1] Dicey: "Law of the Constitution," p. 139.

But, passing over the misleading illustration, let us consider the kernel of the objection. It is that, if State rights are not guaranteed by some limitation upon the sovereign power of the central government, the State so constituted cannot properly be classed as "federal."

Now the essence of a "federal" system is, as we have seen, that "whatever concerns the nation as a whole should be placed under the national government, and all matters not primarily of common interest should remain in the hands of the several States." That is Professor Dicey's own statement of the "general principle" which underlies all federalism. But now we are told that unless a third condition attaches; if the power of constitutional revision—a matter which manifestly concerns the nation as a whole—is not placed outside the control of the national government, then the system is no longer "federal," but must, apparently, be classed as unitarian.

It should be remembered that this device of an ultimately supreme constituent assembly is not peculiar to federal governments. It is found in constitutions, such as those of France and of Belgium, which are indisputably unitarian. It is not typical of any form of government. It is adopted in federal and unitarian constitutions alike when it is desired to make the basis of the constitution difficult to alter.

The assertion, therefore, that a constitution, apparently federal, in that it provides that State affairs shall be regulated by State assemblies, is not in reality federal, because it makes the national assembly supreme, among other things, on the question of constitutional revision, may be safely denied. But if it were not so, if it should be deemed that the casuist has the advantage in verbal definition, and that such a form of government cannot properly be deemed federal, the repulse need not concern us greatly. If a form of government achieves a solution of urgent political problems, questions of nomenclature may be left to take care of themselves. We may safely say with John Locke, "so the thing be understood, I am indifferent as to the name."[1]

We may conclude, then, that it is dangerous to attempt to lay down any hard and fast rules as to the inevitable consequences of a federal system of government, and that it might be possible that, under certain conditions, a form of government having all the advantages of federation might gradually be evolved without developing either a written constitution or a constituent assembly outside and controlling the federal assembly.

Let us consider whether it is not conceivable that such an evolution might take place amongst

---

[1] "Civil Government," chap. 12, § 146.

a people who, like the inhabitants of the United Kingdom, have developed their constitution slowly, during the course of centuries, and who are acclimatised to the operation of custom and understandings as formative constitutional forces.

To aid this consideration, let us take an illustration of the manner in which the formative influence of custom has been applied to the constitution. In theory, until quite recent years, the House of Lords was the court of final appeal from English courts of justice. Every member of that House was, by right, entitled to sit and vote upon every case which was brought up to the Lords for decision. But when, in course of time, those cases became more numerous and complex, it was manifestly inexpedient that they should be decided by a large body, the majority of whom were innocent of any legal training. The custom therefore arose of leaving the law lords to deal with them without interference from the lay members of the House. Those law lords constituted the House of Lords for the special purpose of hearing appeals. Any other member of the House possessed the technical right of voting, but an understanding sprang up that they should not interfere, and the advantage of the understanding was so manifest that it gradually grew into custom; and the influence of the custom became so strong that when the O'Connell case came up on appeal, offering severe political temptation to the lay lords to interfere with the decision of their legal brethren, it had force enough to restrain them.

The reader is asked to imagine that the relations between England, Scotland and Ireland had been of such a character since 1800 that a somewhat similar self-denying ordinance should have appeared reasonable; that it should have seemed expedient to members of the House of Commons that they should not interfere in questions which in no wise affected their own particular nation. That such a state of affairs is not inconceivable is proved by the case of Scotland. At times there has been a distinctly discernible tendency to permit the Scotch members to settle small matters of national importance. The "Scotch night" is an institution not altogether unknown to the House, when its rafters reverberate only to the melodious accents of the north country. If the occasional had become the customary, an Irish Municipal Corporations Bill might have been passed by a House composed solely of Irish members, and a Church Disestablishment Bill might have been rejected by English votes alone. The understanding might gradually have grown into a custom so strong in its constitutional influence that no member would have dreamt of violating it. Just as a decision of the law lords alone was in fact the decision of the House of Lords, a "State" bill passed by the Irish, Scotch or English members alone would have been in fact a bill passed by the House of Commons. The change would have been effected by custom solely; not even a resolution of the House would have been necessary to give it validity.

It must be distinctly understood that it is not contended that this silent change could have been effected in the actual circumstances; it is only contended that such relations might have existed between the three kingdoms as would have made the change possible. Nor could it have been effected without a corresponding change in certain other constitutional understandings, more especially those which relate to the resignation of ministers in certain events. But a readaptation of all these practices might have taken place without the violation of any law, and consequently without the necessity for passing any Act to regulate them.

Let us suppose, then, that this silent change had been completed by 1850, and that when any State question was under debate in the House of Commons, the representatives of the two States which were not interested in it were to be found habitually in the smoking-room or at their clubs. At about that time, as we have seen,[1] Parliament

---

[1] See *ante*, p. 63.

would have become fully conscious that it was overwhelmed with work, and members would be casting about for a remedy. It would not take them long to recognise that a great waste of time was going on, and that an enormous economy would be effected if all the States business were transacted concurrently instead of postponing the work of two of the States while that of one was being considered. The remedy would be so simple and so effectual that it could not fail to be adopted. The members for each State would meet at certain hours of the day, under the presidency of a deputy speaker, and at a given time they would resolve themselves into the Imperial Parliament for the consideration of national affairs. And this second change would involve no infraction of any written law of the constitution, and could be effected by simple resolution. A second stage in the journey towards practical federation would have been reached, but it could not have been reached unless the members for each State had exercised an amount of political foresight, moderation and forbearance which is not easily acquired. The limits of State rights would have been defining themselves slowly by practice, and this evolution could not have taken place unless the State sections of Parliament had rigidly adhered to a determination not to attempt to deal with questions which could upon any interpretation be construed as "federal," and therefore properly within the purview of the united House of Commons.

The third stage would be reached when Parliament became convinced that it was a useless waste of time and energy to compel the attendance of Scotch and Irish members in London for the transaction of State business, and that such business would be more efficiently conducted in Edinburgh and in Dublin. That conviction would probably be accompanied by another conviction that the efficiency of Parliament would be further increased if it were not compulsory that the State representatives should be also the federal representatives. At this point constitutional legislation would become necessary. An Act of Parliament would have to be passed creating States assemblies, and defining their powers in more or less general terms. The Act might or might not include a reform of the Imperial Parliament, involving a reduction of representatives. Such an Act of Parliament would be a constitutional law, but it would be a misuse of terms to define it as a "written constitution." We should have arrived, by a process of evolution, at a system of government which presented all the essential advantages of federalism, and which did not involve the creation either of a written constitution, or of a constituent assembly which should limit the sovereignty of the Imperial Parliament.

Having thus arrived at a form of federation in which there is neither a written constitution nor a constituent assembly, hard to call together, but which is the only sovereign power competent to revise the constitution, the objection that federalism necessarily involves a "rigid," as opposed to an expansive, constitution falls to the ground. There is no "sovereign despot, hard to rouse," no "monarch who slumbers for years."[1] The Imperial Parliament remains the sovereign controller of the constitution, "the ever-wakeful legislator." In its hands lie the powers of revision, either by expansion or contraction, of the limits of State rights. The flexibility of our constitution is in no way impaired.

It follows also from what has gone before that the second alleged essential to a federal system, namely, that each government, whether federal or State, is a non-sovereign law-making body, is not absolutely true. It is true so far as we have carried our imaginary procedure in regard to the States assemblies, which derive their powers from the Imperial Parliament, but it is not true, as we have already seen, of the Imperial Parliament itself.

We turn, therefore, to the third alleged essential—the existence in the courts of justice of a power to decide whether the Acts of the

Dicey: "Law of the Constitution," p. 140.

federal and of the States governments are valid within the terms of the constitution. Now since there is no existing rigid constitution controlling the Imperial Parliament as developed in our imagined process of evolution, it is evident that there could be no conflict of law in regard to the Acts passed by the Imperial Parliament. That Parliament remains the supreme guardian of the constitution. But there may arise, it will be objected, a conflict of law between the Acts of the States assemblies and the federal law. Those assemblies may, probably will, pass bills which transgress the limits of States rights, and which trench upon federal rights. In that case the duty of deciding upon the validity of a State statute must necessarily be imposed upon the judiciary.

Many objections have been urged against conferring such a power upon judges.[1] It is important, however, to ascertain whether the exercise of that power is inevitable before we go to the trouble of considering them. If the conditions can be avoided, the consideration of the objections will be superfluous. Now it will have been noticed that in the foregoing imaginary evolution of our system of government from an apparent unitarianism into federalism, or quasi-federalism, the House of Commons only has

---

[1] Dicey: "Law of the Constitution," p. 149, *et seq.*; and "England's Case against Home Rule," p. 185.

been mentioned. The question has doubtless arisen ere this in the mind of the reader, "What has happened to the House of Lords? Have the States assemblies become unicameral?" The answer is, that nothing has happened to the House of Lords. The imagined process of devolution would not have affected that portion of the legislature.[1] During the period when the House of Commons was developing the custom of permitting States members to control States questions, and also during the period when the States representatives in the House of Commons were working concurrently, all bills would of necessity have gone up to the House of Lords, and through them to the Crown for the Royal assent. But another function would naturally have been slowly developing in the House of Lords, namely, the function of scrutinising State bills with a view to deciding whether they actually dealt with questions which related solely to the affairs of the particular State which demanded the legislation, or whether, by oversight or by implication, they trenched upon matters which should be treated federally. If the House

---

[1] It is necessary to guard here against the supposition that I intend to imply that the House of Lords, as it is at present constituted, would be efficient for the performance of the functions which are about to be attributed to it. The fact that Lord Salisbury can publicly declare that the House of Lords would not "attend to the opinion of Ireland" (see *ante*, p. 203) is in itself sufficient to negative it. But the question of the reform of the House of Lords is not germane to the present issue.

of Lords came to the conclusion that the bill was not a purely State measure, it would become its duty to send the bill back to the House of Commons for re-consideration. This could easily be effected by an amendment striking out the clause which limited the operation of the bill to the particular State in question. The bill would thus become a federal bill, and would necessarily come under the cognisance of the whole House of Commons. It is assumed throughout this argument, as it was assumed in regard to the House of Commons, that the Second Chamber would exercise its functions in a spirit of moderation and forbearance, and, above all, in a judicial as opposed to a party spirit; that it would be actuated, in fact, by a sincere desire to give effect to the will of the States so far as was compatible with federal interests.

Now when the third stage of the supposed evolution was reached—that is, when the States sections of the House of Commons, not necessarily composed of the same persons as the State representation in the Imperial Parliament, met in the State capitals—the procedure in regard to bills would still remain unaltered. The States assemblies would continue to send up their measures to the House of Lords, and that House would consider, in the first place, if they were in fact purely States bills under the terms of the statute which created the States assemblies. If the Lords decided that they were States bills, they would proceed with them in the ordinary course; if they considered that the proposed legislation was federal in its scope, they would send it down to the Imperial House of Commons.

By such a course of procedure every bill, whether State or federal, which received the Royal assent would become an Act of the sovereign Parliament, and would appear in the Statute-book as such. There would be no variation from the present practice. State legislation would not be the work of a non-sovereign law-making body which might be treated in the courts as invalid because it infringed some federal law. The judiciary would not be called upon to decide any such question, because all statutes would "be enacted by the Queen's most excellent Majesty, with the advice of the Lords spiritual and temporal and Commons" in Parliament assembled. The judges would doubtless have to consider whether a given Act of Parliament repealed by implication some portion of an earlier Act; but that is a difficulty which is constantly occurring at the present time. The question whether the repealing Act arose in the first instance in a States assembly, and the repealed Act in the Imperial House of Commons, would not affect the decision of the judge in any degree whatever, for all Acts would be equally statutes of the realm.

We have seen, then, that it is possible, in certain circumstances, to conceive the growth of a form of government which offers all the main advantages of federalism, and which is not encumbered with any of the drawbacks which are supposed to be inherent in it. It is true that under the imagined system the national government would remain the supreme law-making body, and therefore capable of revising the constitution, even to the extent of diminishing or abolishing the State assemblies. It is true also that the theoretical jurist refuses to class such a constitution as "federal" in the strict sense of the term. That fact need not disturb us if the constitution in question conferred all the benefits which are attendant upon federalism. We have seen that the adoption of some such system would satisfy a proved need of the United Kingdom. In a nation like our own, which is accustomed to see constitutional questions settling themselves by custom and by understandings, which is inured to the existence of constitutional powers which are rarely or never exerted, the fact of the existence of such a control need trouble no one. If the system worked well, the power of revision would remain merely a reserve force; if the system worked ill it would afford a speedy remedy.

CHAPTER XVI

THE BALANCE OF GAIN AND LOSS

The general aspects of federalism have now been considered, together with the objections which can be urged against it in comparison with a unitarian system of government. The conclusion which has been reached is that those objections, although they are founded upon a comparative observation of existing forms of federalism, are not based upon conditions which are absolutely essential to every form of it; or, to state the case more accurately, in view of the contentions of the theoretical jurist, we have found that it is conceivably possible to establish a form of government which would confer all the admitted advantages of federalism without at the same time entailing those drawbacks which are alleged to be inherent in the system.

Before dealing with the specific objections which have been urged against the adoption of federalism as a form of government for the United Kingdom, it will be well to note how completely the development which we have imagined would remedy the evils which have been demonstrated to exist in our present constitution. There must needs be objections which can reasonably be urged against any form of government. None can be ideally perfect; no ingenuity could devise a constitutional machine which would have no weak point in its construction. All constitutional reform depends upon a balance of advantage and disadvantage, and the aim of the prudent reformer is to adjust the mental scales with accuracy. Let us consider, then, the advantages which would have been gained.

We have already ascertained that Parliament from sheer pressure of business has, for many years, been incapable of transacting all the work which has been demanded of it; that this pressure has arisen from the demand of England, Scotland and Ireland for separate attention, and more especially from the demand of England; and that the urgency of this demand of the separate States has been detrimental to Imperial interests, and chiefly to those interests which are involved in foreign and colonial affairs.

Now it must be evident that the adoption of some system of government analogous to federation would at once remedy all these evils. The work which is now done in sequence would be transacted concurrently by four assemblies. There would be no conflict between the State representatives for a limited and inadequate share of parliamentary time. The affairs peculiar to each State would be regulated by the State assembly. The Imperial Parliament, relieved of a vast burden of petty and local affairs would be free to devote its whole time to the consideration of those large problems, so vital to the welfare of the Empire, which are now too much neglected.

But we have noticed also a second category of evils. We have seen that in consequence of the huge disproportion of State to federal questions dealt with by Parliament, the doctrine that the governed, through their representatives, shall assent to the laws which they have to obey, is being rapidly destroyed. The doctrine which, for good or evil, is the very basis of every well-ordered democracy, is pushed aside, and the majority is not infrequently coerced by the will of the minority. We have also noticed that these conditions tend to divest parliamentary representatives of responsibility to their constituents, and that they foster the growth in Parliament of small political groups.

Again we find in federalism a remedy for these evils. The first, and by far the most serious of them is absolutely done away with. By the relegation of purely State questions to State assemblies, the consent of the majority, through their representatives, to the laws which they will have to obey, is finally established.

By no possibility can the will of the majority be overborne by the votes of persons whose constituents will not be affected by the determination upon the matter in question, and who are in consequence free to regulate their votes with a view to other considerations. The fundamental doctrine of democratic institutions will be vindicated. And, in consequence, as members of Parliament will have no opportunity of voting upon any question which does not concern the nation which they represent, their direct responsibility to their constituents will be re-established. Each member of a States assembly will deal only with States questions; each member of the Imperial Parliament will deal only with federal questions which affect the interests of all. Further, the tendency to form groups in the Imperial Parliament, which militates so strongly against stability of government, would be to a great extent checked. The grouping of members is very largely caused by divergences of opinion upon social questions, most of which would be relegated to the States assemblies. Upon the large problems which would occupy the attention of the Imperial Parliament there is but little tendency to scission; the lines of demarcation hardly admit of the existence of more than two great parties. The exclusion from the Imperial Parliament of those questions which most frequently disturb the political equilibrium would therefore tend, not only to a more deliberate consideration of Imperial problems, but to a more continuous administration of Imperial affairs. The formation of groups, if it took place at all, would be found in the State assemblies, where it would be less injurious, as government by party would in the State be of less importance. It is probable, however, that it would not be found very strongly developed even in the State assemblies, because grouping at present depends very largely upon the desire of the groups to insist upon State interests which are neglected under the present system.

Thus the main evils under which we now labour would be remedied by the adoption of federalism. We must now consider whether that form of government would entail other evils which would outbalance the advantages gained from it.

Some of these evils have already been considered. We have already dwelt upon the disadvantages supposed to be entailed by a written constitution, a constituent assembly, and the interference of the judicature, and we have seen that there is a strong presumption that these difficulties might be overcome by merely following a line of reform which is indicated by our present constitution, and by making only such changes as were absolutely necessary in order to effect the object in view. This class of objection has been developed to a considerable extent, but since it can be avoided, there can be no need to follow it into all its ramifications of detail.[1]

Another objection, which has not been covered by the argument in the preceding chapter, is that federalism of necessity weakens the federal executive as well as the legislature. This objection is even stated in the extreme form of asserting that "the executive authority must be placed beyond the control of a representative assembly."[2] In other words, the government must of necessity be an extra-parliamentary government, and its rise and fall must not depend upon the vote of the Imperial or any other Parliament. If this were so, if the price to be paid for federalism were inevitably the creation of a bureaucratic administration, we might well hesitate long before adopting it. It would be a poor exchange for the assertion of States legislative rights to acquire a position in relation to federal administration which would resemble that of Grattan's Parliament. It is unlikely that any Englishman, Scotchman or Irishman would consent to a change which rendered the Imperial Government independent of the control of their representatives. But when the argument upon which the assertion has been founded is approached, we find that it is the comparative argument once

[1] See "England's Case against Home Rule," p. 168.
[2] *Ib.*, p. 175.

more. Because the United States, Switzerland and the German Empire have adopted the plan of an executive which cannot be displaced by the vote of a representative assembly, therefore the United Kingdom, if it accepts federalism, must of necessity adopt a similar plan. The answer is that the circumstances of the United Kingdom are entirely different from the circumstances of those countries. Parliamentary control of administration is the outcome of a series of historical events which have no parallel in the history of the United States, or of Switzerland, or of Germany. It may perhaps be safely asserted that this control has never been developed in any other State, although it has been imitated by several. Parliamentary control of the executive is a peculiar outgrowth of our constitution. Some more forcible argument than that from analogy must be produced to prove that the adoption of a policy of federal devolution must of necessity result in the destruction of that control; more especially when it is remembered that it never at any time existed as a factor in the constitutions which are cited as illustrations.

But beneath the exaggeration lies a certain substratum of fact. At the present moment the House of Commons absolutely controls the administration. " The condition of the army, the management of the police, the misconduct of a judge, the release of a criminal, the omission to arrest a defaulting bankrupt, the pardon of a convicted dynamiter, the execution of a murderer, the interference of the police with a public meeting, or the neglect of the police to check a riot in London, in Skye, or in Tipperary, any matter, great or small, with which the executive is directly or indirectly concerned, is, if it takes place in any part of the United Kingdom, subject to stringent and incessant parliamentary supervision, and may at any moment give rise to debates on which depend the fate of ministries and parties."[1] These words state the fact picturesquely, and no more than the fact. It may be that it is neither conducive to the dignity nor to the efficiency of a congested House of Commons that it should burden itself with so much detail, but such absolute power is not without its advantages. Now it is clear that if legislative power were conceded to State assemblies some corresponding executive power would have to be conceded with it. Let us consider a typical case. It will be admitted that, granting the possibility of devolution in any form, the control of local government would of necessity be conceded to the States assemblies. The systems of local government differ essentially in each of the three kingdoms, and they are administered by separate departments. The result of federation in this case would be that the Irish

[1] "A Leap in the Dark," p. 3.

Local Government Board would be removed to Dublin, and instead of having the Chief Secretary for president, it would be presided over by a president with a seat in the Irish State assembly, who would be controlled by the votes of that assembly. In the same way local government would be separated from the department of the Secretary of State for Scotland, and would be placed under the control of a president, who would be responsible to the Scottish State assembly. The present president of the Local Government Board would become a minister of the English State assembly, and in consequence questions relating to local government would disappear from the purview of the Imperial Parliament. Parliament would retain the right of discussing, if it desired, questions relating to local government, but it would not control them; nor would the fate of "ministries and parties" depend upon the result, because the Imperial Ministry would not be responsible for the action criticised. In such circumstances it may be safely assumed that these questions would be rarely or never raised in the Imperial Parliament. The States assemblies would be left to deal with them, and the fate of States presidents of the Local Government Board would depend upon the issue. To that extent the sovereignty of the Imperial Parliament would have been limited. It would have delegated its functions, legislative and administrative, to the States assemblies. Would this be an evil? The question can only be answered by a consideration of the matters which are brought before Parliament in relation to local government administration. If they are usually weighty, involving questions of great national importance, it might be an evil that the control of the Imperial Parliament should be withdrawn. Let the reader test the question for himself by taking down at hazard any recent volume of "Hansard" and reading the reports of the proceedings in relation to local government. He will speedily convince himself that the vast majority of topics upon which Parliament exercises its sovereign inquisitiveness are of an utterly trivial character. Let us take, as an example, the volume which contains the Parliamentary Reports for the period between February 5th and March 5th, 1894.[1] During that month twenty-two questions were raised which referred to local government.[2] Of these only one could possibly be construed to relate to the whole of the United Kingdom, fourteen related to England, five to Ireland, and two to Scotland. Of these there is scarcely one which is not of purely local and parochial importance. We find parliamentary curiosity excited to know

---

[1] Hansard, N.S., vol. 21.
[2] Public elementary education is not here included within the domain of local government.

why a sick pauper was not permitted to see his friends; whether a healthy pauper was fairly treated; what was the cause of a certain outbreak of measles; why a court-house was so long under repair; whether it was seemly that a girl should dance in a lion's cage; if a local vestry had subscribed out of its funds to a political demonstration; whether a certain doctor had made himself very ill by vaccinating himself with calf lymph; and whether the site chosen for a fever hospital was suitable for the purpose. It may be said without injustice that these problems are typical of the manner in which parliamentary sovereignty is exercised in relation to local government. It can hardly be maintained that the retention of the power to make these curious investigations is bound up with the safety of the Empire or with the sufficient assertion of the sovereignty of Parliament. It might be delegated to State assemblies, not only with perfect safety, but also with great advantage. There is only one question in relation to local government which can be said to affect each of the three States; that is the question of transferring persons domiciled in one State, and becoming chargeable upon the parish in another State, to the parish of their domicile, and in this particular case a unitarian system of government and the sovereignty of Parliament has produced the astonishing result that, while Irishmen who become chargeable upon the parish in Great Britain can be transferred to their Irish domicile, Englishmen and Scotchmen who become chargeable upon the parish in Ireland cannot be transferred to their domicile in Great Britain, but must be maintained out of Irish rates.

It is not contended that all the limitations upon the sovereign power of the Imperial Parliament that would result from any system of delegation which created a federal government would be as inconsiderable as those which have just been cited. In certain cases more serious questions would arise. For instance, the question of the administration of justice is one which, as it will be shown hereafter, would naturally be relegated to the States assemblies. Those assemblies would control the methods of procedure in the courts and the machinery by which judgments were executed. How, it may be asked, could the Imperial government be certain of enforcing its rights? The Imperial Parliament imposes a tax which, let us suppose, is distasteful to the Scotch. People refuse to pay, and they are sued in the States courts. Granting that the judges are unprejudiced, and that the Imperial exchequer obtains judgment, or, in the other event, obtains judgment in the court of appeal, how is that judgment to be enforced? The State assembly may be in sympathy with the Scotch in their objection to the tax, and since they alone control the means of executing the decision, they can easily render it inoperative. The Imperial Parliament would be powerless. No amount of questions, debates, or votes of censure would avail anything. The will of the Imperial Parliament could only be enforced, either by the authority of the army, or by a repeal of the State constitution.

Here we are face to face with a difficulty which is inherent in every form of federation the danger of conflict between the federal and State governments in the matter of judicial administration. It is a danger against which it would be necessary to introduce safeguards. In the matter of recovering taxes it would not, as we shall see, prove insurmountable.[1]

There is a somewhat analogous difficulty, not involving actual conflict between the powers of the federal and States governments, but arising from the possibility that one States assembly might, within the scope of its powers, act in a manner so contrary to the confirmed sentiment of the other States that the Imperial government would be forced to interfere.[2] For instance, let us suppose that legislation in respect to land were delegated to the States assemblies, and that the nation subject to one of those assemblies was opposed to the payment of rent. It is probable

---

[1] See *post*, p. 326.
[2] "A Leap in the Dark," p. 109.

either that laws would be passed which would be detrimental to the landlords' interests, or that the collection of rent would, by the apathy of the executive, be rendered impossible. It is conceivable that the sense of justice of the other two States would be so outraged that interference with the recognised jurisdiction of the offending State would be rendered inevitable. The possibility of such a crisis would seriously impair the stability of the federal system, and measures would have to be adopted to guard against any such occurrence. But although the difficulty is patent, it is frequently pressed to the verge of the ridiculous. While reading the objections which are urged under this head by supporters of the unitarian constitution, one is sometimes tempted to wonder why it is not suggested that one of the States might possibly revert to cannibalism, or adopt the suttee. The unavowed assumption seems to run through them all that the power to do injustice must necessarily be followed by unjust action, even though it were injurious to the interests of the perpetrators. It has been suggested, for instance, that the inhabitants of a State might be tempted to smuggle in order to defraud the Imperial government; that federalism might mean the revival of contraband trade, and that the State government might take no action to suppress it, or might even encourage it.[1] The contention,

[1] "A Leap in the Dark," p. 110.

clearly stated, is that a body of enthusiasts would incur considerable personal risk, and undergo almost certain financial ruin, in order to annoy the federal government. The federal government, if it could not compel efficient supervision on shore, would control the police of the sea. Smuggling is a dangerous and an expensive avocation. It requires large profits to make it worth following. In the days when nearly all goods, both of export and import, were subject to prohibitive and protective tariffs and embargoes, these large profits could be realised. Both the outward and the return journey could be made profitable. But in these days of free trade it is cheaper to export through the ordinary channels of trade than by means of a private vessel which may suffer prolonged delay because it is known to the revenue cutter, and the margin of gain upon the few classes of goods liable to customs which could be imported would yield no adequate return for the great expense incurred. The patriot smuggler would speedily find himself in the bankruptcy court, where, seeing that his enterprise would have been productive of injury solely to certain of his fellow-countrymen, he would meet with scant sympathy. But exaggeration of statement must not blind us to the reality of the objection which is concealed behind it. Any scheme of federation which created a danger that the individual action of one State would revolt the sentiment or the prejudices of the others would be in unstable equilibrium.

The same objection shapes itself in another form. It is urged that it would be impossible to prevent States executives from infringing upon federal rights if the sentiment of the State in question were in favour of such infringement. For instance, it is supposed that, in the case of Ireland, although the control of national defence would be outside the competence of the State assembly, yet the Irish executive might wink at the unauthorised levy of a force which would in reality be an army, and that, during periods of war, it might countenance and support an enemy of the federation.[1] The contingency is possible, but certainly not probable. The argument that it is probable is based upon the very questionable assumption that the hostility of the Irish to the central government, which has been generated because the Irish national wish in regard to purely Irish national affairs has been overborne by English and Scotch opinion, will be permanently continued when the cause of it has been removed. To make the assumption good it would be necessary to show that Irishmen so differ in nature and character from others of the human species that the natural results of the removal of a grievance are in-

[1] "A Leap in the Dark," p. 111.

operative in their case. In other words, we have got back to the old racial argument, or to the mysterious miasmatic influence which is now sufficiently discredited. Nothing is absolutely certain in the political world, but surely the more reasonable presumption is that when the Irish have acquired control of those affairs which peculiarly affect them they will gradually drop their hostility to Great Britain. The process may be slow: the irritation of centuries is not to be cured in a day even by the most even-handed justice. For a time hot-headed politicians may still declaim that "if the demon of war broke out in Europe" the Irish "would march to the tune of the 'Marseillaise,' and not to that of 'God save the Queen.'"[1] But the froth of politicians soon vanishes when it is fed by no simmering of discontent, and when a nation is satisfied it refrains from marching to any tune whatever, and soon comes to laugh at the mere suggestion. Nevertheless, the fact that we must, in the case of Ireland, expect to reap an aftermath of discontent, however righteous and just the federal provisions may be, is a danger which must not be forgotten, and which must, if possible, be guarded against.[2]

[1] The *Times*, October 8th, 1895. (Mr. W. Redmond.)
[2] It will be noted that some of the objections which are considered in this chapter have been urged against the Irish Home Rule Bills of 1886 and 1893, which attempted to create a quasi-federation which was altogether amorphous and illogical.

It is worth while, however, to note that Professor Dicey, after urging the objection at considerable length, confesses that the "topic is too odious, *and too far removed from practical politics*, to need more than the allusion required for the completeness" of his argument.[1]

Another objection which has been urged is that a States assembly which desired a particular policy which it was incompetent to carry into effect might pass resolutions upon the subject, and that these resolutions would have a greater moral effect within the State in question than the federal law which was opposed to that policy.[2] It is suggested, for instance, that the Irish would desire protection for their manufactures, and that, as is most probable, the State assembly would be precluded from establishing it. But that State assembly, although it could not legislate, might pass a strongly worded resolution to the effect that protection was essential to the prosperity of the nation, and that its concession was absolutely necessary. And that resolution would have a greater moral effect than the actual legislation which enforced free trade.

It may be at once admitted that if States

I have endeavoured to separate those objections which might be urged against any form of federation from those which were aimed at special provisions of those bills.

[1] "England's Case against Home Rule," p. 178.
[2] "A Leap in the Dark," p. 83.

assemblies chose to spend their time in passing resolutions which could have no effective value instead of dealing with questions which were by law submitted to their control, if they occupied themselves with stirring up discontent instead of allaying it, such conduct would prove a weakness to the federation. And it is possible that the objection is not merely fanciful. It is conceivable that before the concession to the States of the control of purely State affairs had produced that healing effect which may be reasonably expected from it, the national irritation which had been generated in Ireland by the previous form of administration might lead to some such protest, which would be a demand for State control over a question which was essentially federal. The danger is one against which it would be necessary to safeguard, and it will be shown hereafter that this could be done by making it detrimental to State interests that State assemblies should comport themselves in this fashion.

Another objection is that England as a State would be so overwhelmingly powerful that it would outvie the others "in wealth, population and in prestige."[1] This was originally urged against a federation between Great Britain and

[1] "A Leap in the Dark," p. 124. The word "prestige" is a hateful one, and as applied to England, apart from Scotland and Ireland, it is meaningless; but it is necessary to deal with each argument in the terms in which it is couched.

Ireland, but it may be held equally applicable to a federation between the three kingdoms. It is said that "no one State should be so much more powerful than the rest as to be capable of vying in strength with the whole, or even with many of them combined." The objection seems to ignore the fundamental basis of federalism, which is that "whatever concerns the nation as a whole, should be placed under the control of a national government. All matters which are not primarily of common interest should remain in the hands of the several States."[1] The "wealth, population and prestige" of England would find its natural and legitimate predominance in the Imperial Parliament, which would control "whatever concerns the nation as a whole." No scheme of government for the United Kingdom could affect that predominance: it is based upon unalterable fact. But England, so long as she maintained the predominance due to her "wealth, population and prestige," and also controlled, through her State assembly, her purely State interests, would not desire to interfere with the action of the State assemblies of Scotland and Ireland unless they either (1) acted in a manner which was violently repugnant to the English sense of justice, or (2) attempted by resolution to trespass upon the domain of federal affairs. If these two

[1] Dicey: "Law of the Constitution," p. 134.

dangers were avoided, the "wealth, population and prestige" of England would not be stirred to antagonism. The precautions, therefore, which are admitted to be necessary to guard against those two evils, would also obviate any difficulty which might arise from the predominant influence of England.

A somewhat analogous objection is that the State assembly of England would deal with so vast an array of interests that it would necessarily attract to it all the talent and administrative genius of the country: that it would become the dominant assembly, and that the Imperial Parliament would be a body of secondary importance.[1] No doubt if the result were that one State assembly acquired such a predominance that it attracted to itself a greater amount of respect and esteem than the Imperial Parliament, the efficiency of the federal government would be greatly injured. But the whole question depends upon the limitations which are to be established between the federal and the States assemblies. That is a question which can only be accurately determined when those limitations are more specifically considered. It will then be seen that they necessarily leave so large an area of jurisdiction to the Imperial Parliament that the objection would be found to carry but little weight. It has arisen to a great extent

[1] Hansard, vol. 341, c. 704; 4th Series, vol. 32, c. 546.

from recent parliamentary exigencies which have resulted in the practical squeezing out of that large section of imperial affairs which relate to foreign and colonial policy. Federalism would restore those questions to their legitimate position in the Imperial Parliament, and it would then be at once seen that the vast and complex considerations which they involve would of necessity attract to that assembly at least as large an amount of ability as those social problems which would come before the English States assembly. They would appeal perhaps to a different class of talent, but by no means to a second-rate class.

Another objection, which must not be passed over in silence, arises out of the peculiar distribution of political opinion in Ireland. It is called "the Ulster difficulty." The term is misleading, because the area of difficulty is limited to a portion of Ulster only. In that district opinion is strongly against the adoption of any form of Home Rule for Ireland, and, it may be assumed, would be as strenuously opposed to any form of federation. It is contended that, when opposition to government is concentrated in a particular area, especially if that area contains a population possessed of more than the average of wealth and enterprise, although that population may constitute but a small minority of the State, government by the State can never prove successful. Either the poor and apathetic majority will tyrannise over the energetic minority, or the minority will attempt to free themselves from the burden of the State authority by force. In the particular case of Ireland, the difficulty is accentuated by a difference of religion, which widens the cleavage between the contending parties. We should be blinding our eyes to facts if we asserted that these fears had no foundation, and even if they had none, the mere existence of them could not be prudently left out of account. Whether the dread of that portion of Ulster to which the argument applies that it would be governed tyrannically by the Irish State assembly would ever be fully realised may perhaps be open to doubt. It assumes that there would be no re-formation of parties in that assembly; that the Nationalist-Catholic party would cohere. Recent events have not in any way tended to strengthen such a supposition. It is, on the whole, more probable that the creation of a State assembly would at once split the Nationalists into Moderate and Progressive parties, and that the Unionist portion of Ulster might find salvation in adherence to the former —might even dominate its policy.[1]

But, in essence, the objection is, after all, merely a specific instance of a more general

[1] I have found this opinion entertained by Irish Unionists—in private. It is not, of course, expounded by them upon the public platform.

objection which has already been admitted. The danger is lest the Irish State assembly should so act as to offend the English and Scotch notions of justice and decency. The safeguards which will have to be imposed to prevent the federal constitution from being endangered by such a course of action will be effectual for the specific purpose.

Another objection which to the readers of the foregoing pages will seem somewhat fantastic, is that it is absolutely impossible to distinguish between federal and State business.[1] It will be well to consider it in the exact words of its most distinguished exponent. "Whatever Ireland ought to ask for in principle, Scotland has a right to ask for in principle. I accept that entirely. And whatever Ireland has a right to ask for in principle, Middlesex has a right to ask for in principle, and whatever Middlesex has a right to ask for, Yorkshire has a right to ask for. That I entirely grant. . . . I should be glad to know on what basis a distinction is drawn between Yorkshire and Middlesex on the one hand and Ireland and Scotland on the other."[2]

The cases of Yorkshire and Middlesex were evidently selected with a purpose. They happen to be two of the very few counties in England

---

[1] Hansard, vol. 335, c. 117.
[2] The Right Hon. A. J. Balfour.—Hansard, vol. 335, c. 110. See also 4th Series, vol. 22, c. 1313.

for which public-general Acts have been passed.[1] But if separate columns for these counties had been opened in the analysis of legislation which we have considered, they would have been almost a blank, and their percentage of legislation would have been represented by an almost inappreciable decimal. The distinction in principle is that, while Middlesex and Yorkshire have no interests whatever which are distinguishable from the interests of the other English counties, Scotland and Ireland have many and important interests which are distinguishable from those of England. If a man passes from Surrey into Middlesex he is governed under exactly the same laws, unless he purchases a piece of land, in which case he will be compelled to go through an extra formality. If he were to go from Northumberland to reside in Roxburgh, he would find himself subjected to a different code of laws in most relations of life. The inhabitants of Middlesex and of Yorkshire are not, except in the rarest instances, subjected to legislation which they alone have to obey, by the votes of the representatives of other English counties. The Irish frequently, and the Scotch at times, are subjected to such legislation by English votes. The distinction in principle is clear and indisputable.

[1] The "Duchies" of Cornwall and Lancaster are other cases in point.

The last objection which has to be noticed is that "Federalism is at least as likely to stereotype and increase the causes of division between England and Ireland as to remove them."[1] This objection was urged against the Home Rule Bill of 1886, and although Professor Dicey was dealing with the question of "Home Rule as Federalism," he was mainly arguing against the provisions of that bill, which could only be called federal if the word were used in a most elastic sense. The whole question is treated as if the demand for federation were an Irish demand, and that the granting of it could only be injurious to England. The present investigation has been an attempt to show that the question is not merely an Irish, but a national one; that each of the three States would gain solid advantages from federation. If, therefore, it could be conclusively proved that the causes of difference between England and Ireland would not be removed, the argument for federation would not be thereby demolished, it would only be weakened.

What, then, are the grounds for the assertion that federation would stereotype the causes of difference between England and Ireland? The first is one which we have already had to consider, namely, the assertion that there does not exist in Ireland the sentiment which makes for

[1] Dicey: "England's Case against Home Rule," p. 178.

federation, that the Irish feel no loyalty towards the Union.[1] In order to enforce this argument, Professor Dicey makes the following remarkable statement: "If such a government is to be worked with anything like success, there must exist among the citizens of the confederacy a spirit of genuine loyalty to the Union. The 'unitarian' feeling of the people must distinctly predominate over the sentiment in favour of 'State rights,'" and he founds upon that alleged necessary condition to federation the argument that it could not succeed in the case of the United Kingdom, because the Irish sentiment in favour of State rights predominates over their "unitarian" feeling. But, in the sentence quoted, Professor Dicey the partisan is speaking, eager to make a point against his political opponents. When Professor Dicey the astute lawyer and keen-sighted jurist is addressing his pupils at Oxford, he tells them, as we have seen, quite a different tale. He informs them that we may perhaps "say that a federal government will hardly be formed unless many of the inhabitants of the separate States feel a stronger allegiance to their own State than to the federal State represented by the common government."[2] That is the mature and unbiased conclusion of the impartial and scientific investigator, which the

---

[1] Dicey: "England's Case against Home Rule," p. 178.
[2] "The Law of the Constitution," p. 133. See *ante*, p. 226.

eager politician ignores. The opinion of the Professor is to be preferred to the contradiction of it by the partisan. Both assertions cannot be upheld by any series of verbal gymnastics.

The second ground is that Nationalists believe that local self-government will bring wealth and prosperity to Ireland; and that the belief is a delusion. The inevitable re-awakening will cause the Irish to lay the blame upon the federation, and their dissatisfaction will be increased.[1] It is much to be doubted whether any such general belief is held by the advocates of Home Rule. They do not anticipate that a miracle is about to be worked, and that the mere creation of a State assembly will endow Ireland with wealth and prosperity. If any such conviction were current, the considerations which were submitted in our historical retrospect of the condition of Ireland must convince us that it is chimerical. The process of restoring to Ireland even a moderate amount of national prosperity must needs be exceeding slow. But for national prosperity, there is an inevitable condition precedent, and that is, national content. If a nation is permeated with a conviction that the law under which it is governed is merely organised injustice, even though that conviction be absolutely baseless, national prosperity is an impossibility. The people become listless and

[1] Dicey: "England's Case against Home Rule," p. 183.

apathetic, caring only for the needs of the moment. Let them obtain control of their own affairs, and this impediment is at once removed. There is opportunity, at any rate, for a recrudescence of energy. Nothing is more fatal to the development of Irish prosperity than the constant and appalling drain upon the population which is caused by emigration. A man is a more valuable national asset than an ox; his necessities create a greater amount of commercial activity.[1] And every man who leaves Ireland, quits it, not from choice, but on account of a fixed belief that under present conditions a tolerable existence is not possible for him. Until that belief is eradicated, until the Irishman knows that his future lies in his own control, the very elements which make for success are wanting. Give him the necessary ground for content, and then, although prosperity may be slow of approach, and although the character of that prosperity may never be identical with the commercial prosperity of Great Britain, yet it will neither be, nor appear to be, unattainable. The Irish will then see the national problem in its true perspective, and not through the dis-

---

[1] I recently heard a large landowner who was considerably interested in the trade of an Irish country town, lamenting over its decay. "For every five people," he said, "whom we fed, clothed and housed twenty-five years ago, we now feed, clothe and house only two." For the facts relating to Irish Emigration, see Lough: "England's Wealth: Ireland's Poverty," chap. v.

torting medium of unremedied grievance, and it is quite an unproved assumption that they will then blame the federal union for failing to achieve results which it could in no circumstances contribute to produce.

The result of this part of our inquiry, then, is that we discover five objections to the federal system as applied to the government of the United Kingdom which may be reasonably raised:—

1. That there is a danger of conflict between the federal and States executives which would be inimical to good government.

2. That States governments might weaken the federation by action within their legitimate powers which might offend the sentiments of the other federated States.

3. That States executives might endeavour to infringe upon federal affairs.

4. That States assemblies might endeavour to achieve by resolution objects which they were precluded from attaining by legislation.

5. That States assemblies might ignore the rights of minorities.

It will be seen that all these objections, except perhaps the first, are based upon fears which may or may not be realised. Nevertheless, it is the duty of the legislature to guard against possible and contingent evils. It will also be seen that they are based in fact upon only one assumption, namely, that States assemblies and executives will act, within their spheres of power, unreasonably. The safeguard which will be an effectual preventive of unreasonable conduct in one direction will be equally effectual in all; and to the creation of such a safeguard it will be necessary, when the proper time comes, to direct our attention.

CHAPTER XVII

FEDERATION *VERSUS* HOME RULE

It is not the purpose of this investigation to deal directly with the questions which have been raised by the Government of Ireland Bills of 1886 and 1893. Home Rule for Ireland is not federation in the proper sense of the term. It is an anomalous political adjustment which might solve an urgent political problem for a time, but which must lead in the end to a complete system of federation. Such of the objections to the Home Rule Bills as can be also urged against a scheme of federation have been considered and appraised in the foregoing chapter. But there are objections to certain provisions of the Home Rule Bills which cannot be urged against federation, and the advantages of the latter system cannot be completely demonstrated unless this fact is taken into consideration.

The main objections to the Home Rule Bills of 1886 and 1893 were:—

1. That they abolished the effective supremacy of the Imperial Parliament.
2. That it was not practicable or just either

to exclude the Irish members from the Imperial Parliament, or to retain them in it.

3. That the bills were unjust to England (and Scotland), because they did not give her control of her own State affairs.

4. That our present system of Cabinet government would be destroyed.

5. That a new and dangerous factor would be introduced into our constitution by the power conferred upon the judicial committee of the Privy Council to decide upon the validity of Irish legislation.

6. That the proposed financial arrangements between the two countries were unsatisfactory, and would be productive of discord.

7. That the restrictions upon the Irish State legislature and executive were insufficient, and would prove inoperative.

With many of these objections we have no further need to deal. We have seen that the sovereignty of the Imperial Parliament must, to a certain extent, be delegated, and, to that extent, limited, and we have admitted that this delegation might in certain circumstances give rise to a conflict of authority which would threaten the well-being of the constitution, and that therefore precautions must be taken to prevent the provocation of such a conflict. We have seen also that federation, by giving England the sole control of her State affairs, removes the third objection. We have examined the arguments which are supposed to show that federation means the sacrifice of our present system of Cabinet government, and we have found them singularly inconclusive. We have discovered that there is a possible method of securing the advantages inherent in federation without necessarily introducing the judiciary as a factor in determining the limits of the constitution.

The chief objections to the financial arrangements of the two Home Rule bills were, first, that they were unjust to England; and, second, that, since Ireland's contribution towards imperial expenditure was in the nature of a tribute, it would be certain to cause dissatisfaction in Ireland, and would prove a sure cause of conflict between the federal and the State governments. These objections are not founded upon principle; they are merely assertions that certain financial proposals are inexpedient. They do not weaken a single argument against federation; they merely attack one method of carrying out a detail of the federal scheme. If the objections can be maintained, there are other possible arrangements which would avoid them.

The objections based upon the supposition that the restrictions upon the power of the Irish government would prove inoperative, have already been partially considered. We have admitted that precautions ought to be taken against any infringement of the State executive upon federal reservations, and also against any attempt by the State assembly to extend its sphere of operations by the moral force of resolutions. Another objection is that the restriction which is represented by the power of the Lord Lieutenant to veto bills is valueless. It is contended that he must exercise that power either upon the advice of the Irish executive, which will be in harmony with the views of the majority of the Irish State assembly, in which case it would never be put in force, or it must be exercised upon the advice of the imperial cabinet, in opposition to the wish of the Irish executive and assembly, in which case an acute conflict between the State and federal governments would at once arise.[1] There is no valid answer to this objection; but the fault is inherent in that one-sided and anomalous form of quasi-federation which is termed "Home Rule." A scheme has already been foreshadowed in which, by a natural adaptation of the existing constitution, the question of creating a new power of veto upon States legislation need never be raised.

But the question around which controversy raged most violently was the position of the Irish members in the Imperial Parliament. The promoters of the two bills were fully conscious of the extreme difficulty of the problem. At one

[1] "A Leap in the Dark," p. 93.

time or another they favoured each of the three possible solutions. In 1886 they advocated the exclusion of the Irish from any representation in the Imperial Parliament,[1] except in certain events for the purpose of altering the provisions of the bill.[2] In 1893 they first proposed to grant Ireland a reduced representation in the Imperial Parliament, subject to limitations which were intended to prevent them from voting upon any bill or motion relating solely to Great Britain.[3] In the bill, as presented to the House of Lords, the limitations had disappeared, and the reduced Irish representation was permitted to vote in the House of Commons upon all questions, whether federal, Irish, English or Scotch.

There is no fourth solution of the difficulty possible under any scheme of Home Rule for Ireland, and against each of the three insuperable objections can be urged. The proposal to exclude Ireland from representation in the Imperial Parliament, except for purposes of revision of the Irish Government Act, would, in fact, create a constituent assembly which would be the constitutional sovereign in the place of Parliament. It would unnecessarily introduce into our constitution many of the disadvantages which are entailed by such an assembly. Furthermore, such a relation of Ireland to England would be a

[1] Government of Ireland Bill, 1886, sect. 24.
[2] *Ib.*, sect. 39 (b).
[3] Government of Ireland Bill, 1893, sect. 9.

direct negation of the first principle of federalism. It would indeed concede to Ireland the control of those matters which related purely to the State of Ireland, but it would deprive her of any control over all federal affairs which involved the interests of the whole of the United Kingdom, except those which related to amendment of the Act which granted her self-government. On all the vast and complex questions which are and must remain federal and which must be dealt with by the Imperial Parliament, the voice of Ireland would be for ever silent. She would not be in the position of a member of a federation: her status would be that of a dependent State, controlling its own purely State affairs, but governed in all other respects by an irresponsible dictator. It has been argued that Ireland would gladly accept this position in consideration of Home Rule, and that it would be well for her that she should do so, in order that she might devote her undivided attention to purely State problems. Irishmen may think thus at present, but it is well-nigh impossible that the opinion should be held permanently. If prosperity were attendant upon the grant of Home Rule, Irish interests would become involved to a greater extent than at present in the larger federal problems, and the Irish would increasingly desire a fair influence in the solution of them. If prosperity followed but slowly upon the attainment of Home Rule, or appeared unlikely to follow it, the Irish might with every semblance of reason allege that this disastrous result was consequent upon their exclusion from all voice or vote in relation to Imperial questions. Such a form of mock federation could never permanently solve our present constitutional difficulty. It is opposed to the true federal idea.

These objections were pressed strongly home upon the authors of the bill of 1886. They were so conclusive against the total exclusion of Ireland from all participation in federal affairs that in 1893 the proposal was abandoned in favour of the scheme popularly known as the "in-and-out clause," which retained a reduced Irish representation at Westminster for federal purposes, but excluded it from interference in affairs which related solely to Great Britain. The device was ingenious, and it avoided some of the more manifest drawbacks which would be entailed by total exclusion. No shadowy constituent assembly would have been created: the supremacy of Parliament over the constitution would have been maintained. Ireland would have retained her fair share of control over federal affairs. England and Scotland together would have obtained conjoint control over their State interests. The Imperial Parliament would have been at one moment the federal assembly and at another the State assembly of Great Britain.

If a patchwork federation could by any means prove efficient, this clever device might possibly pass muster as the best of a bad series of proposals. It is the nearest imitation of federalism which could be devised. But it would have entailed consequences which are little less than grotesque. Let us imagine that the system had been in operation at the commencement of the Parliament of 1892. The vote of want of confidence which overturned the Salisbury Government was a federal question, and the Irish members would have legitimately taken part in it. But when Mr. Gladstone's Government had been formed it would have been competent for the leaders of the Opposition to formulate a motion amounting to a question of confidence, which was manifestly "confined to Great Britain or some part thereof," let us say, to Scotland. The Irish members could not "deliberate or vote" upon that question. The Government would have found itself in a minority of about 40, and according to all constitutional custom, would have been bound to ask for a vote of confidence, to resign, or to dissolve. The vote of confidence, being federal, could have been easily obtained, but the first question which subsequently arose in relation to Great Britain would have ensured a second defeat. It needs little argument to prove that our methods of government could not remain permanent in such circumstances. We should either have to submit to the serious disadvantage of rapidly-changing ministries, or we should have to permit the upgrowth of a custom that Government should not resign in consequence of defeats upon questions relating to Great Britain. Either alternative would be injurious. The latter would mean the practical sacrifice of parliamentary control over the administration. And even if it were admitted, it would not prove effectual. No such custom could extend itself to serious defeats upon bills relating solely to Great Britain or some part thereof, and such a defeat would have been an absolute and immediate certainty. Besides, in other conditions it might be possible that Government would have the confidence of Parliament upon questions affecting Great Britain, but find itself in a minority upon Imperial affairs when the Irish vote was admitted. It may be said with absolute certainty that no such arrangement could prove permanent. It would not be practicable even if the greatest amount of forbearance, good sense and toleration were exercised by members of the House of Commons. Continuity of government could only be maintained by a persistent sacrifice of convictions and of political promises, a condition which could never be realised, and which, if realised, would prove disastrous.

It is not surprising, therefore, that, during

the committee stage, the clauses excluding the Irish members from participation in the affairs of Great Britain disappeared from the bill. In the amended bill, as presented to the House of Lords, the Irish representatives were entitled to deliberate and vote in the Imperial Parliament upon all questions, whether federal, English or Scotch. It is inconceivable that the supporters of the bill can have regarded such a provision as a permanent settlement. They must have viewed the whole of the Government of Ireland Bill merely as a provisional arrangement pending the creation of a proper federation. For while the State affairs of Ireland were freed from the domination of irresponsible votes, the irresponsible voting power of Ireland in relation to the State affairs of England and Scotland was stereotyped and accentuated. Whenever a British question came before Parliament it would be liable to be decided, not by the majority of British members, voting under a direct responsibility to those who would be affected by the result, but by such a majority as might chance to form itself according to the distribution of the Irish vote between the two parties. It is probable that in many cases the distribution of that vote would lead to the transformation of the British minority into a majority, and the great evil which has been considered at length in a former chapter would be perpetuated.[1]

[1] See *ante*, p. 87.

But, it may be urged that the Irish, having obtained control over their own State affairs, would naturally confine their attention to federal questions in the Imperial Parliament, and absent themselves when British affairs were being discussed. It would not be to their interest to meddle causelessly with British questions, and so call down upon themselves the anathemas of British electors. Prudence and good sense would dictate abstention. The assumption is of more than doubtful probability. The Irish members would naturally fall into line with British parties upon purely federal questions. Upon those questions the British minority, reinforced by an Irish contingent, might constitute a majority of the House. The Irish members who formed part of that majority would desire to keep the Government in office. They would perceive that if they abstained from interference in British questions, they would leave the Government in a minority. Those British questions would have no interest for their constituents, whereas the maintenance of the Government in power might be of paramount importance to them. It would be inevitable then that they should persistently support the Government upon British questions, and that the opinion of the British majority would be habitually over-ruled.

Thus we perceive that each method which has been proposed for solving the federal problem under a system of Home Rule is so fraught with constitutional danger that it is rendered impossible as a permanent arrangement. It is said by many that Home Rule is, after all, only a stage upon the journey towards federation; that the English character demands that constitutional reforms shall be taken in sections, and that it is well to commence with reform at the point where the need is most urgent. All this may be admitted. Every reform has been accomplished by slow degrees, and it is not probable that the reform now under discussion will be achieved at one stroke. The road towards federation will be journeyed slowly, and it is well that the progress should be slow. The fault of the movements of 1886 and 1893 was that they were made down the wrong road.

CHAPTER XVIII

CONCLUSION

THIS inquiry is approaching a conclusion. The only subjects which remain for consideration are, first, what are the proper relations of the States assemblies to the Imperial Parliament; second, what are the natural and reasonable limits of the powers of those assemblies; and third, by what methods should the change be effected. These are subjects which need only be touched upon lightly. To analyse all the minute details of the machinery by which federation must be brought about would be too long, too tedious, and too intricate a task. The purpose of the inquiry has been to establish the urgent need of reform in the direction of federalism. If that purpose has been achieved the details of the measure may be left to the administrator and to the parliamentary draughtsman. It is only possible here to consider the question in its broadest aspects.

In an earlier part of this investigation we allowed imagination to conceive how, under favouring circumstances, an informal but practical federation might have gradually emerged from our present unitarian constitution.[1] We found that the ultimate result would have been the evolution of three States assemblies, dealing with the purely State questions of each nation, which would have been, in fact, mere delegations or offshoots of the House of Commons. They, together with the popular chamber in the Imperial Parliament, would have been executing the functions of the old House of Commons. They would, in fact, have been an integral portion of the Imperial Parliament itself. The essential unity of the system would be exemplified and enforced by the fact that States as well as federal bills passed through the House of Lords to receive the Royal assent, and thus became as completely "statutes of the realm" as States Acts are at the present time.

Following this suggested line of natural evolution, we come to the conclusion that any federal system which would be adapted to the peculiar needs of the United Kingdom would consist of an Imperial Parliament composed, as at present, of two chambers and the Crown, and three States assemblies, which would consist of one popularly elected chamber. For our purpose the creation of a State "second chamber" would be either anomalous or superfluous. A second elected chamber would be anomalous because it

[1] See *ante*, p. 250.

would, if it differed from the first upon any State question, merely raise a contest as to which set of electors expressed the will of the State—a contest which, from its very nature, could never be decided. A non-elected second chamber would be superfluous because the second chamber in the Imperial Parliament would be already fulfilling that function.[1]

The Imperial second chamber would then form the federal bond of union in matters pertaining to legislation. Its natural duty would be to examine judicially and impartially all States bills which were presented to it, with a view to ascertaining whether they in any respect exceeded the powers committed to the States legislature, or infringed any federal provision of the constitution. This would by no means involve the creation of a written constitution in Professor Dicey's acceptance of the term. Portions of our constitution are already written. The Act creating the States assemblies might preclude them from legislating in a sense contradictory to these, or some of them. Let us suppose, for instance, that they were precluded from any legislation which infringed the provisions of the Bill of Rights. Let us also suppose that a State assembly sent up a

[1] I assume throughout the existence of a second chamber which would exercise its functions in a judicial, impartial and non-political spirit. I have endeavoured to indicate how such a second chamber might be brought into existence in "The House of Lords: a Retrospect and a Forecast."

local government bill which contained a clause empowering municipal authorities to search Protestants for arms, and to deprive them of them. This would be a clear case of a State assembly exceeding its powers. The duty of the second chamber would be to reject the obnoxious clause and return the amended bill to the State assembly. If that assembly accepted the amendment, the subsequent progress of the bill would be as at present.

But we must now suppose the case of an assembly persisting in such a clause after it had been rejected by the House of Lords, and the more serious but less probable case of a States bill which was in its entirety an infringement of federal rights. In those cases the House of Lords should hold that the State desired deliberately to raise a federal question, and it should be incumbent upon them to refer the bill to the Imperial House of Commons, which alone would be capable of dealing with it. We may, perhaps, go a step farther and say that the powers of the second chamber in relation to States bills should be limited to guarding the rights of the federation; that when it was satisfied that a States bill did not exceed the powers of the States assembly which presented it, the House should be *functus officio*, and should not be entitled to reject the bill on its merits.

It will be seen that thus, by very slight constitutional change, a system having all the advantages of federalism might be evolved out of our present form of government. The system would provide an immense incentive to the States assemblies to act with caution and moderation within their allotted spheres. They would know that the moment they attempted legislation which trenched upon federal rights, such legislation would be subjected to considerable delay, and, if persisted in, would finally be relegated to the Imperial House of Commons for consideration. The States assemblies would be, in fact, mere offshoots of the House of Commons for the purpose of dealing with particular States questions.

But, it may be urged that, although the proposal might work well in the case of States which were anxious to preserve the efficiency of the federation, it would be a mere provocation to naughtiness if any State felt itself irked by the limitations placed upon State rights and were desirous of forcing more extended concessions. In that event the State assembly would persist in sending up to the second chamber bills which were in excess of their powers and, when they were amended, or referred to the Imperial House of Commons, would provoke a national agitation which would be fatal to the good working of the system. It is, of course, conceivable that a State assembly might forego a present advantage in order to secure what it deemed an ultimate gain, and it is also conceivable that the electors of that State might permanently support their representatives in that irreconcilable attitude. The assumption may be illustrated thus. The Irish are above all things eager to secure a reform of Irish municipal government. Their State assembly has power to deal with the subject, but (let us assume) it has no power to legislate in the matter of education.[1] The Irish resent the limitation, and, to accentuate their objection, they pass a municipal government bill which (among other clauses) places the control of education under the municipal boards which their bill proposes to create. This is an infraction of the constitution. The House of Lords throws out the clauses relating to education, and returns the bill to the Irish assembly. That assembly re-inserts them, and the House of Lords, acting within our imagined constitutional practice, refers the bill to the Imperial House of Commons, where it is subjected to delay and possibly to rejection. Now in that event how would the members of the Irish assembly have to present their case to their constituents? They would

[1] It must be distinctly understood that this is merely assumed for the purpose of the illustration. It must not be taken to imply that education is not a proper subject for State control. The point will be made clear when the methods by which the change to federalism should be effected. See *post*, p. 311.

have to say, "Here is a bill for which you have earnestly longed, and which, in the main, might have been enacted during the present session. But it is a sin and a shame that we can't control the question of education, and, to mark our abhorrence of that incapacity, we have suffered our municipal reform bill to be wrecked. You must go on living under a system of local government which you dislike until we can wring from the Imperial Parliament the right to legislate upon education." It may appear probable to some minds that a State assembly would act thus, and would be permanently supported by the opinion of the State electors. It is merely a repetition of one of the objections to federalism as a form of government for the United Kingdom, founded, as I believe, upon unjustifiable fears, which have already been considered, and against which a safeguard is necessary. The nature of the safeguard will be described later on.[1]

It must be specially noticed that the proposed plan entirely eliminates the judiciary as a factor in the constitution. No court of justice could ever be called upon to decide upon the validity of either a State or a federal Act of Parliament. Every Act would be an Act of the Imperial Parliament, and no conflict of law could by any possibility arise. The supremacy

[1] See *post*, p. 333.

of Parliament in respect to legislation would not be affected in the slightest degree.

We now have to consider the natural and reasonable limits of the powers of the States assemblies: that is to say, we have to ascertain the subjects of legislation which, under existing conditions, and assuming the smooth working of the federal organisation, would naturally come under the control of the States assemblies. In order to arrive at the basis of fact upon which the claim for self-government of each of the nations composing the United Kingdom could be founded, the legislation of the Imperial Parliament since 1801 has been analysed into federal and States legislation. For the present purpose it is necessary to carry that analysis a step further, and to distribute that federal and State legislation into categories in order to ascertain upon what subjects Parliament has been compelled from the very nature of our institutions to adopt separate State Acts.

The tables opposite give the facts. The figures for each decade represent the yearly averages.

Two facts at once become apparent from a consideration of these tables. First it will be noticed that the decadal average in the categories tends on the whole to diminish, especially since 1850, with the exception of the rapidly expanding class of public locals. This fact is

CONCLUSION

1.—FEDERAL.

Date.	Revenue.	Army, &c.	Militia.	General Administration.	Constitution.	Trade.	Factories, &c.	Co-operation.	Offences.	Religious Disabilities.	Justice.	Land.	Property Law Reform.	Church.	Poor.	Local Administration.	Traffic.	Education.	Public Local.	Total.
1801-10	1.9	3.5	.7	7.5	.5	8.0	.1	—	1.7	.8	1.1	—	—	—	—	—	—	—	—	25.9
1811-20	8.6	5.1	.9	7.4	.8	9.6	—	—	3.4	1.2	2.8	—	.1	.1	—	—	—	—	—	39.8
1821-30	8.7	3.5	.9	8.1	.3	8.4	.3	—	1.5	1.2	1.2	.2	.4	.1	—	—	—	1.1	—	34.4
1831-40	8.7	2.6	1.9	9.3	.7	6.7	.5	1.1	.9	1.4	1.3	—	1.6	—	.6	—	1.1	—	—	34.7
1841-50	6.2	2.6	2.6	10.1	.4	8.4	2.8	1.0	3.6	1.5	1.7	3.1	.2	—	.4	—	1.5	.4	—	36.0
1851-60	7.9	3.5	1.7	13.4	1.1	4.2	.8	.3	1.6	1.0	1.4	1.1	.4	1.1	1.1	—	1.6	—	.7	35.4
1861-70	6.1	3.9	4.1	10.6	.7	6.4	.5	.9	2.3	.2	2.6	.3	3.1	1.1	.4	.8	.6	—	1.2	41.7
1871-80	6.8	2.8	.1	10.4	.6	4.9	.6	.7	2.0	—	2.1	—	—	1.1	1.1	—	3	.4	1.5	34.5
1881-90	5.1	1.3	—	—	—	4.4	—	—	1.4	—	1.5	—	1	—	—	—	1	—	—	29.0
Average	6.7	3.2	1.3	9.5	.6	6.8	.3	.3	1.8	.9	1.7	.1	.2	.1	.2	.1	.4	.1	.3	34.6

2.—STATES (ENGLAND, IRELAND, AND SCOTLAND.)[1]

Date.	Revenue.	Army, &c.	Militia.	General Administration.	Constitution.	Trade.	Factories, &c.	Co-operation.	Offences.	Religious Disabilities.	Justice.	Land.	Property Law Reform.	Church.	Poor.	Local Administration.	Traffic.	Education.	Public Local.	Total.
1801-10	7.0	—	4.2	12.8	.9	12.9	—	1.7	3.6	.6	6.4	1.7	—	2.6	1.2	3.8	1.2	.4	—	59.4
1811-20	9.0	—	3.3	8.4	.9	14.3	.3	2.9	4.9	.2	9.8	2.7	—	2.8	1.4	7.2	2.5	.3	—	65.9
1821-30	1.8	—	.4	5.0	—	7.8	—	.6	4.2	.5	13.7	2.3	.7	3.3	1.2	7.1	3.5	.2	—	51.0
1831-40	—	—	—	6.3	1.3	9.5	1.1	1.2	2.9	.4	16.9	1.9	1.6	4.1	1.7	16.0	3.5	.5	—	58.5
1841-50	1.1	—	—	.6	1.1	4.5	—	.8	2.5	.3	13.7	3.9	1.6	3.8	3.3	15.2	4.8	2.5	—	63.1
1851-60	.2	—	.7	8.6	2.3	5.4	.1	2.1	1.9	.5	13.5	6.1	1.6	4.3	1.1	18.2	4.1	1.7	4.7	70.3
1861-70	—	—	.1	7.5	1.4	5.4	—	.1	1.7	.2	12.4	5.4	1.1	4.1	2.1	17.9	1.7	3.7	2.6	71.7
1871-80	—	—	—	5.2	1.6	2.3	—	—	1.7	—	9.4	1.6	1.0	3.6	1.0	11.4	1.9	1.7	4.8	70.6
1881-90	—	—	—	4.1	—	2.7	—	—	.7	—	7.0	2.9	—	2.2	.5	10.3	—	—	—	85.3
Average	2.1	—	1.0	7.0	1.3	6.7	.1	.4	2.6	.3	11.4	3.2	.9	3.4	1.5	11.4	2.9	1.3	8.8	66.3

[1] Statutes relating to Great Britain, and to England and Ireland, are excluded.

especially noticeable in regard to the table representing the averages of State legislation. But it must not be on that account assumed that there has been any considerable fusion of State into federal legislation. The assumption is contradicted by the fact that federal legislation has not increased. It is due to three causes, which may be shortly enumerated.

1. In the earlier portion of the century each expiring law was continued by a special Act, which has of necessity been enumerated in its appropriate category. During the later period, all expiring laws have been continued by one Act, which has been classed as federal.

2. The growing tendency to greater comprehensiveness in Acts of Parliaments: to deal with a subject as a whole, in one Act, rather than piecemeal in several.

3. The congestion of Parliament since 1850, which has caused a block in legislation. This has affected State legislation to a greater extent than the federal.[1]

The second and more important fact brought out by the tables is the limit to the power of Parliament to legislate federally. In order to make these limits clear, the categories have been divided into three compartments by thick black lines. In the first of those compartments will be found those topics upon which Parliament

---

[1] See *ante*, p. 62.

has succeeded in legislating federally, or which, from their nature, would be properly reserved to the federal government. In the second compartment will be found those subjects upon which the federal grasp is only half complete. They relate chiefly to trade questions and to offences, and it will be shown presently why it was impossible that Parliament should be able to deal with them in an entirely federal spirit. When we come to the third compartment we find the federal action of Parliament practically paralysed. The first column, which relates to administration of justice, may at first sight appear to indicate an uncertain assertion of federal control, but if this category were analysed more minutely it would be found that the federal Acts related chiefly to what may be termed the administration of external justice, such as consular courts, admiralty jurisdiction, and the like, which would naturally fall under the control of the federal government. So far as the internal administration of justice is concerned,[1] Parliament has never been able to deal with the question as national.

The nearly absolute incapacity of Parliament to deal with these questions from the national standpoint may perhaps be more clearly illustrated in diagram form. In the following diagram the upright columns represent the total average

---

[1] Except those statutes which abolished the death penalty for certain offences. These were federal.

legislation under each category from the date of the Union to 1890. The black portion of the column represents the federal legislation, the shaded portion represents the States legislation.

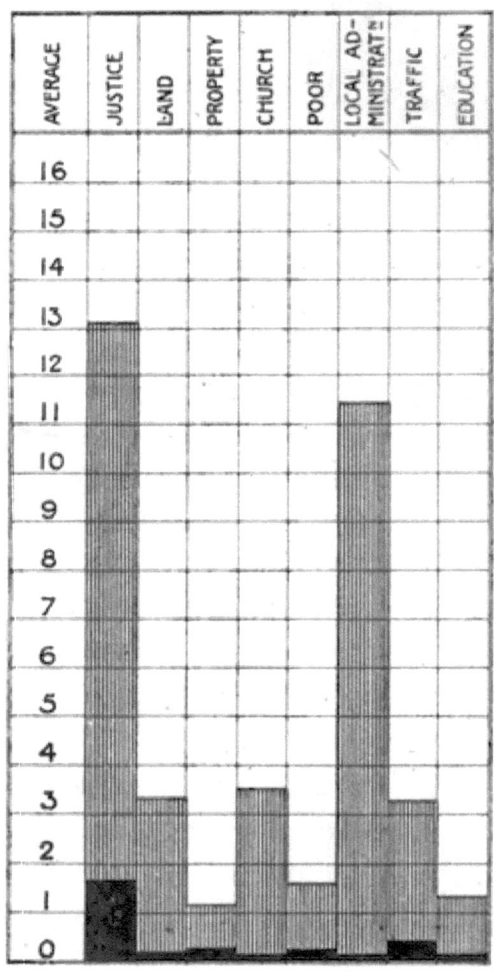

The "public locals" have been omitted, because the public locals which are federal have little or nothing in common with those which affect the States.

It is necessary to mark carefully the nature of the topics upon which Parliament is incapable of legislating federally, for that is not less important than a clear perception of the existence of that incapacity. We find then among these topics :—

1. The administration of justice through the courts of law.
2. The laws relating to the tenure and occupation of land.
3. The law relating to the holding, transfer, and devolution of property (including land).
4. The law relating to the Church.
5. The law relating to the poor.
6. The law relating to local government, rural and urban.
7. The law relating to roads, railways and canals.
8. The law relating to education.

It will be observed that all these subjects touch very closely the every-day life and needs of the people. They are not questions in which any considerable body of men can remain uninterested. With the exception of the law relating to trade, and of the question of taxation, they make up the body of legislation which affects most nearly the social and material well-being of the citizen. They are questions upon which he cannot afford to be apathetic. For good or for evil, his interests are bound up in the right solution of them. And it is precisely in regard to these every-day questions that we find that the inhabitants of the United Kingdom have no community of interest. Each nation desires a different solution of each problem, or, previous to the Union, was so far committed to a different solution that unity of purpose and of action was rendered impossible. The essential conditions of the case preclude even the ultimate attainment of such unity of purpose and action. And it is precisely in regard to these subjects, which entwine themselves most closely with the very fibres of daily existence, that our present constitution permits the will of those interested in them to be overridden by the votes of others who will not be affected by any change in the law.

These subjects, therefore, are those which, in the peculiar circumstances of the United Kingdom, should naturally and properly be relegated to the control of the States assemblies. The claim of the States to control these affairs is indisputable under any federal theory. We now pass to the "doubtful" compartment of our analytical table for the purpose of considering how those topics should be distributed. It will be seen that this compartment contains, in essence, two categories: matters relating to trade, with two expansions, factory law and co-operation; and offences, with the cognate subject of religious disabilities. This latter expansion may be regarded as no longer representing any practical subject for legislation.

The category "Trade" has been expanded into the two other categories of "Factories" and "Co-operation" for the purpose of showing that, upon these subjects at any rate, Parliament has been able to legislate federally. Whether that federal legislation has been an advantage to each of the three States may be a matter of doubt, but the fact remains. In the main category of "Trade" the balance appears uncertain, but a minuter analysis would show, as in the case of "Administration of Justice," that the federal legislation related in the main to questions of "external" trade, such as tariffs and foreign commercial relations,[1] and that the States legislation affected questions of "internal" trade, such as the regulation of markets and of special trades which required special provisions. These latter would naturally come under the control of the States assemblies, while the former would be reserved to the federal parliament.

But against this proposal two objections are certain to be urged from different points of view. It would be monstrous, it will be said, on behalf

---

[1] In respect to trade legislation there is always a difficulty in discriminating between protective measures and "Revenue." Where an Act imposed a duty manifestly for the purpose of protecting a trade, it has been classed in the "Trade" category. The preamble generally discloses the intention of the Act.

of England, that Ireland or Scotland should possess the power of relaxing the provisions of the Factory Acts. By so doing they would be able to release their manufactures from a burden which might still be imposed upon England, and thus practically confer a bounty upon them.[1]

Whatever might be the case in Scotland, there can be little doubt that Ireland, under a federal system, would release herself from the more stringent provisions of the Factory Acts. It would be an interesting subject for inquiry how far the imposition of those Acts, excellently adapted to the necessities of a thriving commercial community, upon a State in which manufactures were struggling and weak, has tended to stifle progress. If our present elaborate code of factory legislation had been imposed upon Scotland, or even upon England, at the end of the last century, the progress of commercial prosperity would most probably have been arrested. It is unfair to impose such restrictions upon a struggling commercial activity, and upon a people striving for an alternative employment to agriculture. If Irish manufactures ever commence to flourish, the workers would begin to demand a similar protection to that enjoyed by workers in England and Scotland. At present they are not able to bear the strain of it. In any case, those who

[1] Hansard, vol. 335, c. 118.

persist in looking at the question from the purely British manufacturer's standpoint, may possess their souls in patience. The British manufacturer need fear no serious competition from Ireland so long as he possesses the coal fields.

The second objection will be urged from the Irish side. "So long as you maintain the right of the federation to deal with questions of external trade, so long you prevent Ireland from reaping the full benefit which local self-government would confer upon her. Ireland needs protection. You refuse her the power to establish it. The abolition of the corn laws largely contributed to the financial ruin of Ireland, by opening to all the world the market for agricultural produce which had been protected for her benefit. Those laws were abolished because free trade was deemed essential to the commercial prosperity of Great Britain. We do not dispute the proposition, we only point out that the external trade policy which is good for England and Scotland may prove Ireland's bane."[1]

There is, unfortunately, too much truth in the contention. But at the same time it would be impossible to concede to the States the

---

[1] There was a considerable amount of evidence to this effect given before the Royal Commission on the financial relations between Great Britain and Ireland.

control of external trade. That concession would involve the right to make treaties with foreign countries, and, in consequence, a separate foreign policy. In no conceivable form of federation could such a concession be made. Even in the highly developed federation of the United States of America, inter-state free trade is guaranteed, and the control of external trade is reserved to the federal government. The concession which might reasonably be made to a mainly agricultural State, such as Ireland, in federation with mainly commercial States, such as England and Scotland, should be, not the sacrifice of control over affairs which are inherent in the federal government, but a reorganisation of State contributions to Imperial taxation upon the basis of the relative population and wealth of the federated States.

The only other category in the "doubtful" compartment is that which is headed "Offences." It is a category which presented considerable difficulty in the analysis. It does not include any statute which creates an offence merely for the purpose of enforcing the provisions of the substantive law which is enacted. The Railway Acts, for instance, created new offences; but that was not their main purport. The creation of the offence was subsidiary to the prime object, namely, to afford increased facilities for traffic. Again, those statutes, so plentiful during the middle of the century, which merely altered the punishment inflicted for recognised offences, are not included. They have been treated as more properly belonging to the category, "Administration of Justice." The present category contains only those statutes of which the prime object was to bring a given act within the scope of judicial punishment, or to remove an act from that scope. It must be evident, therefore, that the power to legislate in that sense upon the subject of offences must be of necessity divisible between the States and the federation. If the State were competent to legislate upon Church matters, it follows, of course, that it could legislate upon the offence of sacrilege. The federal government, having control of external trade, would legislate regarding piracy. The amount of the concession to the States in this respect would be regulated by the amount of local self-government which was permitted.

When we turn to the first compartment, which contains those categories which have been described as essentially federal, surprise may be caused by the fact that, in two of them, States legislation should show so large a proportion. It is clear that the Imperial Parliament has been able to deal federally with the questions of "Revenue" and of "National Defence;" but of the other two categories, "Administration" should, from the relative proportions of State and federal

21

legislation, be classed as doubtful; while the laws relating to the constitution, which should be essentially federal, show a predominance in favour of State legislation.

The statutes which have been classed under the head of "Administration" are those which relate to the conduct of the business of the great departments of government. All Acts which directly relate to the raising and expenditure of money have been classed under "Revenue," but an Act for the better ordering of the national finance, such as the National Debt Conversion Act of 1888,[1] has been placed in the category of "Administration." The same classification has been adopted for all those statutes which relate to the conduct of the great government departments.

Now it is one of the remarkable features of our ostensibly "unitarian" system that the administrative work of government is carried on to a large extent through State departments. We have seen that the whole of the Scotch administrative work is now in the hands of a Scotch Secretary of State, to whose office the Scotch Education Department has been affiliated. In Ireland there is an Irish Secretary's office, a Board of Trade, a Local Government Board, a General Prisons Board, and an Education Department. It was inevitable, therefore, that a

[1] 51 Vict., c. 2.

certain amount of legislation in regard to administration should fall into the States section.¹ Now it is evident that, under any system of federation, a portion of this legislation must necessarily be relegated to the States assemblies. Let us suppose, for instance, that those assemblies were empowered to deal with local government, internal trade, agriculture, and traffic. The State governments would consist of a President of the Local Government Board, a President of the Board of Trade, a Minister of Agriculture, possibly a fourth minister, who would control the railways, navigable rivers, canals, and roads, and a Chancellor of the Exchequer.² Each minister would be provided with a separate department, and the control of those departments must necessarily fall to the State assembly.

The category of laws relating to the constitution exhibits the curious fact that States legislation on this subject is more abundant than federal legislation. This is due in great measure to the fact that franchise and redistribution reforms, although they are usually effected for all

---

[1] I must also admit to a certain laxity of classification in the States section of "Administration," which I did not permit myself in regard to the federal section. I have included a few States statutes, which could only come under that category by straining the definition somewhat. For instance, the State laws relating to marriage have been included in it. This was done to avoid opening fresh columns which would have been useless for purposes of comparison.

[2] See *post*, p. 333.

parts of the United Kingdom with practical simultaneity, are also usually effected by legislation for each State separately. It is also due to the necessity of classing disfranchising Acts, which obviously could only be treated as States legislation, under the head of laws relating to the constitution. But these facts do not afford any valid reason why the question of constitutional reform should not be reserved in its entirety to the Imperial Parliament. That Parliament would be the creator of the States assemblies: it would decide upon the number of members of which they were to be composed, and also the franchise upon which those members were to be returned. That franchise would, upon the theory that the State assemblies were mere offshoots of the Imperial House of Commons, be identical with the federal franchise, and it would not be competent for the State assembly to alter it. By the same analogy the alteration of the numbers of representatives in States assemblies and of constituencies returning them would be solely a question for the Imperial Parliament.

It may be assumed without argument that all questions of national defence would be reserved entirely to the Federal Parliament. The only question, therefore, which remains for consideration is the question of revenue. It will be seen from the analysis that the Imperial Parliament has gained complete control over this department, not altogether to the satisfaction of the minor States.[1] But a State executive must of necessity command revenue for the purpose of carrying on the work of government, and the difficult question at once arises, how should that revenue be raised? Both the Irish Home Rule bills empowered the Irish State assembly to levy any taxes except customs and excise, which were to be imposed and levied by the Imperial Parliament. Two objections were taken to this proposal. The first was that the Irish assembly might act unjustly in regard to the incidence of taxation: that is, that they might overtax landlords or Protestants. The second was that the Imperial Government, having no control over the judicial executive, would find it difficult or perhaps impossible to recover the customs and excise in the face of an apathetic or hostile State government; that in fact the State government could at any time paralyse the federal administration. It is unnecessary to go into the question whether these fears are well founded or not, because a simple device would be effectual to allay them. The main objects to be secured are (1) that the State assemblies should have absolute control over the amount

---

[1] As to Ireland, see Report of the Royal Commission on the financial relations between Great Britain and Ireland. As to Scotland, see Hansard, vol. 335, c. 71, and vol. 341, c. 686.

of revenue to be raised for State purposes, and (2) that the federation should be omnipotent in the collection from each State of such sums as may be decided to be the proper contribution of that State towards federal purposes.[1]

It may be laid down as an axiom that, whatever concessions might ultimately be made to the minor States in respect to the Imperial contribution, the cost of the State government must be entirely borne by the State itself. By no other method could the direct responsibility of the State assembly to its constituents be maintained. The inhabitants of each State must be made fully conscious that the whole of the State expenditure will fall upon their shoulders. That first incentive to economy in State administration is essential. Upon any other system, the poorer States would be in a position indirectly to tax the inhabitants of the richer States, and this would be, not only an injustice, but also a direct provocation to profuse expenditure.

It would be the duty of the State Chancellor of the Exchequer to prepare annually a budget showing the estimated expenditure of all the State departments, and the proposed in-

---

[1] I state the proposition in somewhat vague terms intentionally, because it is not possible to deal here with so large and so technical a subject as the amount of the proper contribution from each State, nor does it come within the scope of this investigation. For an exhaustive account of the financial relations between England and Ireland, see Lough: "England's Wealth: Ireland's Poverty," chaps. iv. and vii.

cidence of the taxation to raise the necessary amount. For this purpose, excise, which relates to internal trade, should be within his control, but customs, which relate to external trade, should be reserved to the discretion of the Federal Government.[1] The State Chancellor would know the estimated produce of customs, and he would allow for it in his budget. When this budget had been accepted and passed by the State assembly, it would be forwarded to the Federal Chancellor for incorporation in the Federal budget. It would not be liable to alteration in the Federal House of Commons; it would be treated as an agreed vote. An addition would be made by the House of Commons for the purpose of raising the ascertained contribution of the State towards Imperial expenses; and the aggregate of States budgets so revised would then constitute the Imperial budget, to be dealt with by the House of Commons just as it is dealt with at the present time.[2] All taxes would be federal, and would be collected by the federal executive. The amount of the estimates of the States governments would be paid by the Imperial exchequer to the State consolidated fund, and

[1] One of the main grievances of Scotland and Ireland is that their whiskies are highly taxed (10s. 6d. per gallon), in effect, by England, which is not a spirit-producing country.

[2] It is assumed throughout the argument that the State contribution towards Imperial expenditure should be fixed upon some fair basis of comparative wealth and population; to be revised, possibly, every five or ten years.

each State assembly would pass its own appropriation Acts.

It will be seen that such a plan would secure several conspicuous advantages.

1. It would concentrate the taxing power in one hand, while at the same time it gave the States full control over the incidence of State taxation.

2. It would compel each State to bear directly the whole cost of its State administration.

3. It would preclude any State executive which might object to the federal contribution from showing apathy in or hostility to the collection of taxation, because, by so doing, it would be cutting off the supplies necessary for its own financial purposes.

4. It would necessitate the minimum amount of change in our existing financial arrangements.

But, it will be objected, the proposal affords no safeguard against an attempt upon the part of any one State to fix the incidence of taxation unjustly. What is there to prevent the Irish State assembly from mulcting an unpopular minority for the benefit of the majority?

The objection is, in essence, one which has been already fully considered. It resolves itself into the general objection that a State assembly may conceivably act with such conspicuous injustice as to revolt the moral sense of other and more powerful federated States. It has been admitted that such conduct would injure the stability of any federal constitution, and that the very fact that such a fear exists justifies the adoption of safeguards against it. These safeguards will be immediately considered, but it must be noticed that the scheme contains within itself a certain check against unfair taxation. It would be within the competence of the Imperial House of Commons, in the event of a glaring injustice, so to regulate the incidence of taxation for Imperial purposes as to afford a practical remedy.

To conclude this portion of the inquiry, we find that in the existing circumstances of the United Kingdom the control of the following subjects of legislation would naturally be committed to States assemblies: the administration of justice, the laws relating to land and other property, the Church, poor law, local administration, traffic, and education. Upon these subjects Parliament has never been able to exercise a federal control, for the simple reason that the interests and laws of the three nations were so diverse that it was impossible. The laws relating to internal trade fall really within the same category, although an analysis has shown a partial federal control over trade subjects by reason of federal legislation in respect to external trade. With these subjects must necessarily pass a control over the law relating to offences in respect to those matters which are regulated by the State assembly, and also a control over administrative law, limited in the same manner.

These subjects would afford the natural sphere of activity for the States assemblies, provided each State were thoroughly imbued with the federal idea and were determined that it should work efficiently. But those, unfortunately, are not the conditions under which the proposal has to be brought forward. England is not yet convinced of the undoubted fact that her own State interests would be more efficiently protected if she had her own State assembly, because, although she resents the control of those interests by Scotch and Irish votes, she can, by exercise of her predominant voting power, at any moment convert the Imperial House of Commons into what is practically an English State assembly. Ireland is so convinced of the injustice of the present system that she is credited with, and perhaps at times feels, a distaste for even the federal connection. England, in consequence, has no confidence that Ireland would exert her State powers wisely, or with justice. This want of confidence has generated a belief in those dangers which have been already admitted to demand safeguards, and may be summed up in the statement that in all probability the State assembly would act absurdly and unreasonably.[1] Now, as that

[1] See *ante*, p. 272.

alleged danger is based upon prophecy, no argument can remove it; its baselessness can only be proved by experience. But, so long as the fear exists, it would be fruitless to approach the English nation with a proposal for federation which corresponded with what has been indicated as the natural line of demarcation. "What!" the average English elector would exclaim, "give the Irish control of the land, the Church, education, and the administration of justice? Impossible. The landlords would be despoiled, the Roman Catholic Church endowed, Protestants would be forced to attend Roman Catholic schools, and would find themselves treated as outcasts in the courts of law. Never!"

All this may be treated as very absurd and ridiculous, but, unfortunately, it represents an opinion which is tenaciously held by a very large number of those who can command an absolute majority in Parliament. It is of no use blinking the fact; the "predominant partner" must be converted if any scheme of devolution is to secure reasonable stability. It is true that a measure of Home Rule or federation may be carried in the House of Commons by an English minority, converted into a majority by the adhesion of a sufficient number of Irish and Scotch members, but such a proceeding would augur ill for the permanence of the reform. A strong party would exist in England hostile to the new system, anxious that it should prove a failure, incapable, even with the best intentions, of giving it a fair chance, and, worse than all, capable, at the next general election, if they could arouse sufficient dissatisfaction in England, of returning a majority against it in spite of the Scotch and Irish majorities. It is useless to fight against facts. No solution of the problem can be attempted with any hope of success which does not carry with it the acquiescence of England, and some assurance that it will be viewed by her with goodwill in its initial and experimental stage.

It is hoped that the foregoing pages have made good the proposition that the essential conditions of the three States which compose the United Kingdom are such as to demand a system of federal government, provided that certain special objections can be overcome. Their aim has been to prove that we are endeavouring to conduct affairs which are in reality federal under the guise of unity, and that certain very serious constitutional evils have originated in that attempt. It has also been shown that a frank recognition of fact would remove all these evils. The only objection we have to encounter is that the preponderant State in the proposed federation has no confidence that the proposed States assemblies will act with moderation and justice.

How is that objection to be overcome? The answer is, by the method which always has, and always will appeal most forcibly to the average English mind: by proceeding by slow and measured steps. Every student of English politics knows that this is a prime necessity in all political progress. It is inconceivable, for instance, that our present franchise and electoral divisions could have been established in 1832. The few men who advocated anything approaching them were looked upon as political maniacs. It took fifty years and three violent agitations to enable the nation to arrive at their ideal. Our first step in the direction of federation must be a very short step. The concessions to the State assemblies must be in respect of those subjects which most peculiarly affect the interests of the States and which are least likely to give rise to State action which would offend the sentiments of other States. We must select in the first instance for delegation the non-contentious business. No one will dispute that local and private business, including the Acts known as "public locals," might be referred to the States assemblies. In addition to this, local administration, traffic, the poor law, and internal trade might also be delegated in the first instance. They are subjects with which each State might deal without involving even the remote interests of the other States to any appreciable extent.

They are subjects which would open up an immense field for inquiry, investigation, and possible reform. And they are subjects in regard to which Ireland and, to a less degree, Scotland complain that the Imperial control has been injurious. Such a delegation would relieve the Imperial Parliament from a mass of detail business, and would leave it free for the more mature and deliberate consideration of the greater questions which are now neglected.

But this plan would by no means satisfy the aspirations of Ireland. True; and that is the concession which is demanded of Ireland on account of England's want of confidence, be it reasonable or unreasonable, in Ireland's capacity to manage her own affairs discreetly and justly. Ireland wants fuller control of her State affairs; the ultimate aim of the Imperial Parliament would be to concede to the States assemblies the control of all those matters which should naturally fall under that control. A certain portion of them are conceded experimentally. If the experiment works well, more control will be granted. The States assemblies will be put on their good behaviour. The more eager they are to obtain greater power, the more careful will they be to use that power which they possess so as not to offend the sentiments of the sovereign body which alone can extend it. They will be on their mettle to show that, in those matters entrusted to them, the vaticinations of the prophets were groundless. It will be evident to them that if they provoke unnecessary conflict with the federal executive, or gratuitously offend the sentiments of the preponderating State, or persist in attempting to pass Acts which are outside the scope of their powers, or endeavour to force the federal pace by passing barren resolutions, or treat minorities with injustice, they will be doing precisely those things which would most effectually prevent the realisation of their hopes. Every inducement would be offered to them to prove by sincere work and just dealing, within the sphere allotted to them, that the trust reposed in them was justified, and that they were deserving of more trust.

By such means the federal scheme might be evolved naturally, in accordance with the proved needs of the States. It would in itself afford an education in political responsibility if any such education were needed. It would in no way sap the sense of loyalty to the federal State where such loyalty existed, and it would tend to evoke it where, from circumstances which have their origin in the past, it may at present lie dormant.

It has not been possible to do more than indicate the solution of the great problem which has been the subject of this investigation. That it still remains a problem urgent for solution, notwithstanding recent events, no one who has given it even a superficial consideration will be prepared to dispute. That it is a national problem, affecting equally the interests of each of the three States, and not merely peculiar to one of them, I venture to claim that I have proved. And, being a national problem which raises issues of the vastest moment, it is one which ought to be removed from the arena of mere party politics. It is in this spirit that I have endeavoured to deal with it, and it is only in this spirit that it can ultimately be solved.

INDEX

ADMINISTRATION of justice, 271
— of legislation, 321
Africa, annexations in, 14
Agricultural produce, Irish, **178, 183**
Agriculture, the new, 142, 192
America, flight to, 185
American colonies, 244
Andrew Fairservice, 137
Arms prohibited in Scotland, **138**
Arms of Scotland, 146
Army, control of, 275
Articles of association, 123
Austro-Hungary, constitution of, 237
Averages of legislation, 35, **49**
— of debate, **70**

BALFOUR, LORD, on union, 153
Balfour, Mr. A. J., on federation, **283**
Baxter, Mr., motion for **Scotch** secretary, 149
Belgium, constitution of, 247
Bill of Rights, 88
Bristol port, 195
British convention, 144
Budget (State), 326
Butter Act (Irish), 187

CAMERONIANS resist union, 128
Campbell, Sir G., on Scotch business, 167
Cattle, Irish, **178**
Caves, causes of, 104
"Celtic fringe," the, 219
Celtic races, 200, 203
Chancellor (State), 326
Charter schools, 192
Church, disestablishment of, 92
Coercion Acts (Scotch), 137
Colonial debates, 77
Colonies, government of, 12
— interests of, neglected, 85
— North American, 243
Commons, House of, debating function of, 67

Comparative politics, **234, 265**
Conscription, 97
Consent, government by, 87
Constitution, elasticity of, **2, 27**
— dangers to, **83**
— **laws relating to, 323**
— remedies, 262
Cork harbour, **194**
Corn laws, 319
Crimean war, debates on, 87
Cross, **Viscount, on States** legislation, 52

DARIEN expedition, **130**
Debates, defined, 66
— analysis of, 70
Denmark and Sweden, 134, **237**
Dicey, A. V., on the duties of members, 25, 56
— on federations, 225, 241, **246, 285**
— on State armaments, 277
— on State rights, 121
Disfranchising Acts, 324
Doctrines of the constitution, 87
Dress (Scotch) prohibited, 138
Duties on Irish goods, 179, 183

EARTH-HUNGER, 184, 193
Education, 109, 192, 308
Eglinton, Lord, and Scotch petition, 147
Election of 1895, **228**
Embargoes, 186
Enclosure Acts, 37
England, legislation for, **39, 42, 53, 58, 62, 91**
— **and federation, 228**
— **and Scotch union, 129**
— control of, **120**
— dissatisfaction of, 116
— preponderance of, 278
— representation of, 122
— share of debates, 75
Exclusion of Irish members, 296

Expediency and law, 108
Exports, Irish, prohibited, 178

FACTORY ACTS, 318
Famine, causes of, 184
"Federal" legislation defined, 35, 310
— debates, 71, 77
— effect of, 97
— nature of, 43, 63, 99
— rights, infringement of, 275
Federation, definition of, 225, 241, 247
— a transitory condition, 234
— is not "Home Rule," 296
— limit of State rights in, 303
— weakness of, 265
— written constitution in, 245
Fencible-men, 139
Fenianism in Ireland, 231
Fergusson, Sir J., on Scotch business, 150
Finance, Irish, 49
— legislation, 53
— of Home Rule bills, 293, 325
— State, 326
Foreign affairs, debates on, 77, 86
France, Ireland's customer, 184, 186, 194
— constitution of, 247
Franchise, extension of, 117
Froude, Mr. J. A., on government, 106, 110
— on Celts, 204

GEORGE III. and royal prerogative, 3
Germany, constitution of, 236
— executive of, 266
Gladstone, Mr., on local self-government, 166
Glasgow, commerce of, 142, 181, 195
Grattan's parliament, constitution of, 212
— powerlessness of, 218
Great Britain, parliament of, 35
— legislation for, 50
— policy towards Ireland, 179, 185
— trade expansion of, 188
Groups *versus* parties, 103
— remedy for, 263

HAMILTON, DUKE OF, 137
Haversham, Lord, on union, 134, 155
Hedge schools, 192
Hemp trade (Irish), 182
Heritable jurisdictions purchased, 141
Holland, constitution of, 133
— war with, 139
Home Rule bills, 291, 325

Huxley, Professor, on the Celtic race, 203

"IN AND OUT" clause, 297
India, government of, 13
— markets of, 188
Indian mutiny, debates on, 87
Infringement of federal rights, 275
Instructions to committees, 68
Ireland, laws of, 11
— and federation, 230
— discontent of, 176
— effects of federation on, 287
— executive in, 322
— **finance** of, 49, 293
— governed by minority, 89
— legislation for, 46, 54, 59
— local government denied to, 205
— over-representation of, 123
— parliament of, 177
— possible effects of earlier union, 194
— share of debates, 76, 79
— trade of, 180, 199
— under the constitution of 1782, 216
— union with, 29, 45
Irish leaders, 211
— members, exclusion of, 294

JACOBITES resist union, 129
Judiciary and the constitution, 242, 254, 309
Justice, administration of, 271

LAND legislation, 272
Landlords, Irish, 184
Law and morals, 108
Lecky, Mr., on racial characteristics, 201
Legislation, analysis of, 32
— by minorities, 100
— of eighteenth century, 38
— Scotch, 33
— State, 311, 329
Linen trade (Irish), 182
Liverpool port, 195
Local Government Board (Scotland) Bill, 152
Local Government Board of States, 268
Log-rolling, 102
London, self-government for, 169
Lord Advocate, duties of, 149
Lord Lieutenant, veto of, 294
Lords, House of, 94
— and appellate jurisdiction, 249
— debate on union (1713), 131
— functions of, in federation, 256

INDEX

Lords, Irish House of, 212
— reject Local Government Bill, 152
Lothian, Lord, on national discontent, 118
— on Scotland, 156

MAJORITIES unfit to rule, 110
Malt tax, 137
Members' responsibility, 101
Middlesex, claims of, to State government, 285
Militia (Scotch), 139
Ministers, Crown's right to select, 3
— State, 323
Minorities, government by, 89, 92, 100, 111
— power of, 281
Morals and law, 108
Motions to go into committee, 67
— for federation, 171
— for leave to bring in bills, 68

NATIONAL Association, the, 146
— Debt Conversion Act, 322
— defence legislation, 321
— party in Ireland, 282
Navigation Acts, 179, 194

OBJECTIONS to federation, 264
— to Home Rule bills, 291
Obstruction, 8
O'Connell, trial of, 250
Offences, 320

PARLIAMENT, importance of, 5
— and the colonies, 12
— duties of, 10
— (Irish) of 1782, 212
— of Scotland, 177
— paralysis of, 8, 57
— supremacy of, 266
— work of, 30
Parliamentary debates, 66
Peace of Paris, 188
Peerage (Scotch), 137
Percentages of legislation, 41, 55
— of debate, 73
Petition of Right, 88
Pitt, policy of, 144
Poor law, differences in, 270
Porteous riots, 137
Portugal and Spain, 134, 237
Poyning's law, 208
— superseded, 214
Protection, Ireland's demand for, 319
Provisional orders, 48

QUESTIONS in Parliament, 269

REBELLION of 1715, 137
— of 1745, 138
Redistribution Act, 117
Reform in Scotland, 145
Regency question, 216
Rent-raising, 184
Representation, reform of, 122
Resolutions (States), 277
Responsibility of members, 101
Revenue legislation, 321, 324
Revision of constitution, 247
Revolution of 1688, 88

SALISBURY, Lord, on State rights, 121
— on House of Lords, 203, n.
— on Scotch Secretary, 155
Schools (Scotch), registered, 138
Scotch law, 102
— political instinct of, 157
Scotland, laws of, 11
— coercion of, 137
— legislation for, 39, 42, 53, 59, 90
— militia of, 139
— parliament of, 32
— representation of, 142
— share of debates, 76
— social condition of, 126, 195, 196
— struggle of, for federation, 167, 229
— union with, 29
Second chambers for States, 304
Secretary of State (Scotland) abolished, 141
— bills for, 153
— demand for, 146, 149
— result of appointment of, 160
Scott, Sir W., 145
Security, Act of, 129
Seeley, Sir J., 193
Seton, Mr., of Pitmadden, on union, 133
Sheep, Irish, 179
Sinclair, Sir J., and agriculture, 142
Small Notes Bill, 145, 233
Smuggling, 273
Spain and Portugal, 134, 237
" States " legislation, defined, 35, 310
— effect of, 98
— inevitable, 52
— amount of, 50, 314
— business, difficult to distinguish, 283
— debates, 80
Statutes, classification of, 37, 47
— federal, 258
Supreme constitution, 243
Sweden and Denmark, 134, 237

Switzerland, constitution of, 133, 235
— executive of, 266

TAX RIOTS OF 1722, 137
Taxation, enforcement of, 271
— federal, 327
Times, The, on Scotch nationality, 146
Trade, Scotch, before union, 130, 135
— Irish, before union, 178, 193
— legislation, 317

ULSTER, emigration from, 183
— against federation, 281
Understandings, growth of, 249
Union with Scotland, 33, 128
— with Ireland, 45, 89
— failure of, 63
Unionists in Ulster, 282

Unitarian constitution, 242
United States, flight to, 185
— constitution of, 236, 243
— irremovable executive of, 266
— trade policy of, 320

VOLUNTEERS (IRISH), 140

WAR OF INDEPENDENCE, 243
Wedderburn, Sir D., on Scotland, 127
— on local self-government, 161
William IV. and royal prerogative, 3
Wool, Irish, 179
Woollen trade, destruction of, 179, 182

YORKSHIRE, claims of, to State government, 283

www.ingramcontent.com/pod-product-compliance
Lightning Source LLC
Chambersburg PA
CBHW031855220426
43663CB00006B/627